Out of Darkness
The Journey to Hope

Bruce Van Dusen

PUBLISHED BY FIDELI PUBLISHING, INC.

© Copyright 2018, Bruce Van Dusen

All Rights Reserved.

No part of this book may be reproduced, stored in a retrieval system, or transmitted by any means, electronic, mechanical, photocopying, recording, or otherwise, without written permission from the author.

ISBN: 978-1-948638-85-2

For information, email the author at
brcvndsn@aol.com

Published by
Fideli Publishing, Inc.

www.FideliPublishing.com

Chapter 1

I'm thinking about suicide, again. I haven't slept indoors in weeks. I know I haven't eaten much of anything for a couple of days. I've had the same pants on for more than two weeks, and I haven't shaved or bathed in well over a week.

I'm hallucinating, again. I keep seeing this Board of Directors, led by God, that keep saying I'm not worthy of help. They seem to want to keep me down in this awful mess I'm in now.

I don't see anything to cause me to hope. Everything I try doesn't seem to have any effect on my condition.

What is my condition?

The doctors have told me for years I have mental illness. I have schizophrenia and alcoholism. I've been taking some pills I received when I stumbled into the San Francisco General Hospital a couple of days ago. Or, was it today? I don't know. I can't seem to keep track of time.

The pills don't help much. They do help clear my thinking some. But, that just serves to remind me of how bad things are.

Things are bad.

I sleep where I fall from exhaustion. I eat in soup kitchens when I can find them. The other day, I got lost and couldn't find the soup kitchen from the address somebody wrote down. I know I walked a long way. I walked for two days, and I don't think I even came close. I wish I could've found that place. I was really hungry.

I did find a park where some people were having a picnic. I hid in some trees and bushes so they couldn't see me. I knew I'd get in trouble somehow if they found me.

I really wanted a cigarette, bad. I hadn't had a cigarette in a couple of hours, and the craving was strong. I was too afraid to ask anyone for a smoke. Although I'm not sure what I was afraid of. I don't think you can go to jail for bumming cigarettes.

At that point I thought of committing a crime. Just a misdemeanor. I knew I could get some food, and a dry place to sleep in jail. Of course, I'd have to fight off the big guys. I knew they would try to take my food and belongings.

Am I going to step in front of that truck that's coming? I've tried suicide three times before, and it didn't work. There was another time I wanted to jump off a bridge. But, I'm afraid of heights, and I couldn't get near enough to the edge to go over.

God is watching me. I need to make up my mind about this. How did I get to this place where death is better than life?

I grew up in a good place and a great time to be an American. It was a small suburb of Chicago in Illinois. Most of the men in the village worked in steel mills and always had steady work. My father worked in a mill and always had work, and regular pay.

My father was a good man. He always did his best at any task, and was tenacious. He was good at seeing things through. He tried to instill in me good character and sound judgment, even though I didn't see things that way. I thought of things more as an endless list of chores.

My mother is also a good person. She has always had the goal of helping her children. The welfare of her family was a driving force, and she was always moving in a Godly direction. She spent many years not knowing why things happen the way they do, but she never wavered from her faith.

My oldest brother is someone who has overcome obstacles and has achieved success. I've learned much from him, mostly what not to do, but good lessons nevertheless. He has shown patience and kindness to me, and that should be noted.

I have other family that have, in their own ways, overcome barriers, too. They live their own lives each day, as the best people will do.

Our collective experience as a family shows us things don't always go as we wish and that some problems can seem unfair. These are the times when it is important to pull together and work all that much harder to maintain Hope.

Memories serve to fuel my future and remind me of paths to avoid. The hard lessons in Life should be cherished, as they are the coal that is under pressure and will become a priceless gem.

As I play in the yard I notice the trees and flowers and how beautiful they are. I see a humming bird, and it speaks to me. It makes me promise not to tell anyone what it says, and I do so willingly. The first thing I do is go inside the house and tell my mom a bird talked to me. I am, of course, promptly disciplined and instructed that birds don't speak.

I am across the street in the neighbor's front yard, and I discover the sound of breaking glass. I think it's a fun sound and begin to break out sections of the neighbor's front window with a small wooden hammer. I am, of course, instructed on the error of this action.

My sister encourages me to pick the cat up by its whiskers. And I do, wanting the approval of a sibling. The cat scratches me badly, and I'm instructed by mom to avoid such behavior in the future.

Playing games in the neighborhood with my friends was always the best of life. We played hard and put ourselves into everything we did with dedication. Back yard football, Pom-Pom, Running Bases, Hide and Seek, bicycle races, kite fights, sand lot baseball, army men, all were so much fun. How could that ever change? Why would it end?

It seemed to me that my friends were thinking badly of me. I thought I knew what they were thinking. And since I didn't like it, I was out to change it.

It was that funky Eskimo coat, the one with the pointed hood. And the clown suit on Halloween, when everyone laughed at me, or so I thought. It was the time I led the class in from recess and led everyone to the wrong room.

It could be that I was extremely smart. I could read before the first grade and math was a breeze. Maybe I was a normal kid growing up and trying to fit in.

Whatever the answer my solution was to escape. At first I escaped through healthy activity and later through self-destructive means. I read books; all day, everyday. I read books that I could get lost in, ones where I could experience exciting and dangerous adventures.

My favorites were racecar driving stories, books on war, fighter pilot stories and the Hardy Boys series. It could be that I began to see that my life would not be what I wanted it to be.

I loved bike riding and especially long trips. I found that my friends didn't like to ride for miles on all day trips. I discovered that I felt more at ease being alone and sought out ways to be alone.

One day, playing street ball, I decided to switch-hit and bat left-handed. I took the first pitch, hit the ball hard and started to run the bases. The ball bounced up into the neighbor's front yard and blasts through their front room window. Everybody scattered in a dozen different directions. I ducked behind a car and tried to lie down on the ground to hide.

There was this one kid who didn't run. He stood there in the middle of the street. The neighbor came out of his house looking for the culprit. He didn't have to look far, the kid in the middle of the street gladly pointed out my hiding spot, and clearly implicated me as the perpetrator. This was not the first window I'd broken, and it wouldn't be the last.

There were some things that I felt set me apart from the other kids. We went to church at least three times each week. The other kids hardly ever went to church. Our family had Bible devotions after each evening meal, and we always had dinner together. I would have fun at church with the other kids, but later, religion would put an insurmountable barrier between my neighborhood friends and me.

My hair was always cut short. This was during a time when long hair was right for everybody. I was always doing battle inwardly with being different. It seemed I always lost, but the inner conflict didn't stop.

I always had to be in by dark in the summer. The other kids could stay out later, and I felt I was missing out. I tried to voice my objections many times, but as my father would point out, I did not live in a democracy.

There were a great many things I didn't like. I seemed to be angry most of the time. But for many years, I could hide the anger and stay out of major trouble.

In the summer, we went to church camp. It was a good day's drive, and I always looked forward to the trip. It was really great to be there, and we usually stayed a week. We all had great fun pulling pranks and playing sports. As I look back, I see that I miss going each year. I have very fond memories of that time.

I say I had much anger in this phase of growing up. I believe my life had contradictions at this point. I would always try to fit in wherever I was. The result of that was a mixed up kid. I tried to fit in at church and all of those activities, and I tried to fit in with neighborhood kids, as I felt this strong urge to be cool. Part of the time I was a good church kid and the rest of the time I was smoking cigarettes and learning to swear. I was so focused on the acceptance of my peers that I would quite often not think things through and would act on what I thought the cool kid should do.

One summer night at the schoolyard, we found a drunk guy behind a building. He was toasted. He was stumbling, and slurring his speech. We thought it was the funniest thing to see.

I handed him a brick and told him it was a phone call from his mother. He tried to talk to the brick, and I thought it was the funniest thing I'd ever seen. Later, the cops picked him up and he threw up in the cop car. I swore that I would never be like that. I'm better than that.

I had my first drink when I was about five years old. It was at my grandma's house during the summer. My aunt had a beer she was sipping on as she sunned herself. When she went inside the house, I snuck a good-sized drink from the bottle. The alcohol had an immediate and negative effect on me.

There was a kiddy pool in the yard with about ten inches of water in it. It suddenly looked like a good place to go diving. I dove head first into the pool and hit my head on the bottom. Of course it hurt, but somehow, despite the pain, it seemed right. I then repeated that dive several times, as my cousin looked on.

I remember my cousin saying that I was acting foolishly. This was not the first time I'd hit my head, nor would it be the last.

The next time I took a drink would be a few years later. I remember getting up on the kitchen counter and taking out the cooking flavorings. There was vanilla extract, rum flavoring and some others, but the common ingredient in all of them was the alcohol. I poured them all in a glass and filled it with milk. I stirred it up, and then drank it. I remember being dismayed that it was not enough to get a buzz from. The stuff tasted terrible; it should have worked.

My drinking career was about to get a boost. A short time after the cooking flavors disappointment, I had a real drinking experience. It would change my view of the world. It would also show me how to fit in with the rest of the kids.

A lot of us kids liked to camp out in their backyards in the summer. It was an excuse to stay up late and run around all night. On this particular night, we decided to experiment with beer. We each scrounged up some change and had an adult get us a quart of beer each. We were on it, and we thought we had the news. This was to be our big night out.

We agreed to wait until after ten to start drinking our beer. We wanted to stay out of trouble, if possible. Shortly after ten we started.

One kid really complained about the taste, and the other kid, while not complaining, wasn't drinking much. I liked the taste and decided to try to drink it as fast as I could. I was able to get a buzz on pretty quickly. I was into this, and it felt great. I was up for anything.

Afterward, we decided to go swimming in the backyard pool. Swimming under the influence was certainly fun. I was able to climb the wooden swing set in the yard dive from the top. This pool was deeper than the kiddy pool from a few years before, but the concept was the same.

I remember becoming aware of God for an instant. The thought occurred to me that I was not mixing well with alcohol. I told myself if I stayed honest, everything would be okay.

I stuck to my guns on that point. I was always honest with myself and could readily admit that I would lie, steal and cheat to get what I wanted. In fact, this honesty would play a major role in my becoming insane.

Later on that night, we got hungry and snuck into the house and grabbed a cantaloupe. We busted it open on a fence post and had a midnight snack. Soon after, I realized that fruit was what Mom had planned to serve for breakfast. I was at a loss about how to fix this problem.

I realized the grocery store on the other side of town was open all night and we could ride up on our bikes over to get a new melon to replace the unlucky one. So, after some conversation about where to get money, we each snuck into our own homes and found enough to pay for a replacement. We then took off for the all night store.

I knew if the cops saw us we were finished, and I tried to explain that. I think the alcohol may have had some effect on our thinking. After some debate, we threw caution to the wind and rode boldly down the middle of the street. We were determined to complete our quest.

We were able to avoid the police and duck the store's clerk. We completed our mission without incident; though my mom did comment on the melon seeming less ripe than it had the day before.

I do remember realizing that under the influence of alcohol I somehow felt comfortable and at ease with my friends. It's too bad I didn't stop with that one night.

Chapter Two

During normal growth, boys start chasing girls, and girls start taking an interest in their fellow man. I should have started taking an interest in girls, but I found a coping mechanism instead.

In my childhood years, I had been very unsuccessful in the normal amount of discovery in the opposite sex. I felt I was not dating material — at age eight or nine, it's easy to blow things out of proportion. I just didn't have any luck with the girls. Sometimes, I felt angry about it, and tended to harbor a grudge. Other times, I would just reason it away, thinking I wasn't physically attractive or not a "popular" guy.

In the summer between eighth and ninth grade, I had several experiences that would change the course of my life. Being that I felt I didn't fit in, and having the onset of symptoms of schizophrenia, I began to make decisions that were not sensible or appropriate.

Until the eighth grade, I had spent time in a private Christian school. The feeling of not fitting in in the neighborhood was so strong that I relentlessly nagged at my father to allow me to attend public school with my neighborhood friends. He finally gave in, and I enrolled in the public high school.

The first thing I did that summer was run away from home. There was a kid up the street who didn't like living at home, and he decided to leave. The only thing holding him back was that he didn't want to go alone. Being a good sport and friend, I decided to go with him. My home life was tolerable, if painful, and I didn't really have any reason to feel I needed to run away. I just thought it would be a great adventure. So, off we went.

I don't think my explanation for this action, i.e. to venture out and see the world, ever satisfied my parents. After all, what thirteen-year-old kid takes off on a walkabout? I think they felt badly due to some perceived failure on their part.

I did make quite a trip of it. After about five days, the kid from up the street and I parted ways. I finally called my parents from Boise, Idaho to let them know I was okay. They were somewhat worried and asked me to come home. Since things were going well enough for me, I decided to travel some more instead.

I eventually made my way into Canada on my sightseeing tour. I was experiencing a lot of firsts during this time. I was also beginning to get the hang of drinking, and how to manage under the influence, though I never got drunk.

I did manage to return home in time for the start of school. I was something of a celebrity with the other kids and this made me feel like I was starting to fit in and make friends. I also discovered a substance that was soon to become my best friend, and eventually rule my life.

Some people say that marijuana is not addictive, and that it is mostly harmless. In my case, it was my coping mechanism. It was the thing in my life that made me feel all right. Some years later, though, it would become my worst enemy.

I remember the first time I smoked pot. After having sworn I would never do drugs, because the grown-ups said not to, I found that to fit in I would have to do it. I don't remember feeling high that first time, but I do remember winning the approval of the other kids.

Shortly after that, I bought my first bag and proceeded to smoke way too much. I was cooked, so to speak. I remember my first fit of paranoia and dry mouth. I also felt completely out of control. I had no sense of balance. Every time I looked up at the sky, it would make me lose my balance. I tried to go home, but that made the paranoia worse. Plus, having the munchies was going to be hard to explain to my mom.

In spite of all the bad feelings from that first few days of using, I felt that my peers accepted me. I also discovered that the euphoria made my uneasiness and awkwardness tolerable. I could manage to ignore the sense of knowing what others were thinking.

During my first semester as a freshman, I found a good way to fit in and feel comfortable. All I needed to do was give in to peer pressure. Consequently, I started smoking cigarettes and cussing like a sailor.

My drug use was inherently different from the other kids'. Most of the others who got high only smoked once or twice a month. And, they would only smoke a little. My use was daily right from the start.

I used the few minutes waiting for the bus in the morning to get high. During the school day, I found ways to sneak a few tokes and keep my buzz. After school, there was just enough time to smoke a little more. In the evening after dinner and devotions, I would smoke a little more to help ease the stress of home life.

During the first semester of high school, our family decided to move. My father thought that living closer to his job would be better. We also moved to a neighborhood he had always liked, so it made him happy. We moved during Christmas break, so that us kids wouldn't miss any school. My parents were soon to discover their little boy was not as well behaved as he appeared.

I was not able to continue to hide my behaviors indefinitely. By this time, I was self-medicating everyday. I didn't feel okay unless I was high. I also had that same set of problems, and dealt with them the same way. I didn't feel like I fit in, I knew what others were thinking and I didn't like it.

By now, I had some experience with what I needed to do to fit in. So, right off the bat, I was getting dope and getting everybody high. I really believed this was making friends. What it was really doing was making an addict out of me.

During the course of my high school years, the thought of quitting or slowing down would come to mind, but I always opted for dope instead of success.

I also drank alcohol on several occasions. It was always in the form of beer. Beer didn't really taste that good to me, but it seemed popular. Drinking was another way for me to fit in. It was also a good way to self-medicate. Just like the drugs, it would be become a rapacious creditor and consume me.

The first time I got drunk was in the summer between my freshman and sophomore years. I made a plan with a couple of other guys. We arranged for a private place, and we got ourselves three six-packs of tall boys. It was our great experiment. I believe having experience with drugs made it easy for me to cross the threshold into hard drinking. I had no real fear of what would happen. I had been high many times, and knew what to expect.

As we began to drink, I noticed the effect was slow in coming. I was used to the rush from drugs. Alcohol seemed to be less potent and not as effectual, so I increased the rate of my drinking. I drank all six beers, and remember helping my friends finish theirs, too. We thought of everything. When finished drinking I got out my pack of gum and proceeded to cover my breath. I also came prepared with cigarettes and a lighter. We were going to do this right.

As I stepped outside, the first thing I did was fall down. I thought this was the funniest thing that had ever happened. I remember my friends thought it was funny, too. I could not keep my balance and I remember not being able to see too well, either.

I lit a cigarette and suddenly smoking became such a pleasure. When I dropped my cigarette, I remember crawling on the ground to find it. I then went into a blackout. I don't remember much for the next few minutes. When I came-to, I was trying to get in the back door of the house. For some reason, I couldn't get the door open — even though it was unlocked.

I rang the bell, and my father let me in. He didn't say anything and I thought that was strange. I thought my condition was obvious.

I stumbled in, sat down, and tried to watch TV. During the show, I tried to converse, but my speech was slurred badly.

Finally, my brother convinced me to go to bed. I agreed with him. Somewhere in the back of my mind, in my lizard brain, I knew that to get caught being drunk was dangerous.

I thought I'd take a shower before going to bed. Cleanliness is always right. The difficulty with this was I could hardly see through the drunkenness in my mind. So, naturally, it didn't work out the way it should've.

Showering was easy, but turning the water off was an unusual experience. For some reason, my hallucinations were so bad I couldn't see to turn off the water. I turned the knobs this way and that, but couldn't get the water shut off.

Finally, I got one of my brothers to come in and turn the water off. For some reason, he found it hysterical that I couldn't work the valve. I was done showering, so off to bed I went.

I got dizzy as I climbed the stairs, and at the top, everything inside my stomach came out. I braced myself against the wall, and had my first experience with wretched drunkenness. I was a disaster. I accidentally knocked my sister's picture off the wall and threw up on it, as well as my clothes. So, it was back to the shower I went.

Once again, I couldn't get the water turned off. And once again, I had help. My clothes needed attention, as they were pretty messy. So, I went off to take them to the washer and dryer.

I didn't stop to think that I was naked as I did this chore. As I ran through the kitchen, I encountered my sister. She was quite taken back at my appearance. She also got a good laugh when I tried to hand her my clothes, and then asked her to take them to the laundry. She refused and just stood there, laughing.

I ran the clothes down myself. And then I ran back up the steps and discovered the vomit was right where I'd left it. I made an attempt to clean it up, but I was having trouble. I faded out and don't remember the next few minutes.

I do remember being in bed, sleeping, when I was suddenly awakened and pulled upright. I was still pretty loopy and could hardly see. What I heard was my mom's voice asking if I had been drinking. I said no, and was immediately introduced to the frying pan on my forehead. She asked several times and as I repeated my answer she repeated hitting me. I heard my father's voice say, "Stop! You're going to kill him!"

I then passed out and was unconscious for some time. When I woke late the next day, I was sick, and thought I was near death. Again, I denied drinking and stood by that unwaveringly. I was messed up.

I couldn't wait to get back with my buddies and go drinking again. For the next few years, when I drank I drank to get drunk. I was unaware of the deadly effect this would have on my life.

I didn't stand much of a chance with the girls. My religious upbringing taught abstinence until marriage. My way of thinking was that girls were there for sexual fulfillment. As a young teen, my thinking did not go beyond that. And, I was a heavy drug user. Consequently, I didn't have much of a dating life. I was usually so high that the girls thought of me as nuisance instead of a possible date.

Wanting to get high came before everything, and I do mean *everything*, literally. As I look back, I can see this. At that time, I could only think of what I wanted and myself. Drugs clouded my thinking and distorted my perceptions to the point that I didn't realize the bad shape I was in mentally, emotionally and spiritually.

Schizophrenia was in my brain, so physically I was at the beginning of a downward spiral. It was a spiral that would take me to the depths of despair and humiliation.

As a child, I often thought I would be rich and successful. My dreams seemed reasonable and logical. I thought that life just sort of worked out, and everything would fall into place. But that's as far as it went. I think my mental problem didn't allow me to realize that I needed to be more specific about my goals.

I have many mixed memories about my high school years — probably just like everybody else. There were times when things were okay, like when I had enough dope. I'd like to say that I played sports and excelled at academics, but I didn't. I do remember, however, remember some unusual circumstances.

By my junior year in high school, I had already been expelled from a private Christian school. I attended this school for four years before getting kicked out. This school was for the fifth through eighth grade. During those years, I maintained good grades and had friends. But, by the time I was ready for the ninth grade, I rebelled until my parents agreed to let me attend public school. I was headed for trouble right off. I thought the guys who broke the rules and did what they pleased were the right crowd. So, I did what I had to in order to fit in.

There were times when I'd forget my locker combination and would have to find someone to open my locker — usually a custodian. I believe the custodians thought there was something wrong with me. Other times. I would write the combination on the inside of a folder. The problem with that was I would lose the folder or forget where I'd left it.

One really good friend let me use his locker. All I had to do was meet him at the locker when he opened it, but I'd usually forget what time I was to be there. When he discovered I was keeping my drugs in his locker, I was no longer able to maintain that arrangement.

Doing drugs as heavily as I did required money. I was a cigarette smoker, too. That meant even more money. I had a few schemes I used to get funds on a regular basis. Schoolbooks cost money, and losing the book meant you had to buy a new one. I lost my history book six times one semester. The reason it was my history book was because it was the most expensive of the books. Doing this meant I could get my money in one shot. This scheme was short-lived after my parents decided not to buy books anymore.

I also used my lunch money to buy joints before school, and would smoke them before going to class. I would get really hungry sometimes, and my friends got tired of buying me food. Eventually, I had to choose between food and dope. Sometimes, I didn't eat.

Eventually there were investment opportunities. I could buy some pot at a good price, repackage it in smaller amounts and sell it at a higher price. This was usually the best deal for me.

By this time, I was so messed up in so many things that even when I was innocent, people assumed I was guilty. Not only did I get blamed for *my* wrongs, I caught heck for what other people did, too. I think a couple of the guys figured they could set me up for the fall to cover their owns tracks. It worked, too. I was always in some kind of trouble.

My parents were at their wit's end. They tried everything thing they could think of to help me.

Unfortunately, my addiction was not treatable with conventional methods. What I needed was a psychic change. That change would not come for many years.

My parents contacted the local police and asked them for help with me. I had to meet with an officer to discuss my future. He was friendly enough and seemed to be sincere in his endeavor. I thought he was doing fine, right up to the point where I was offered a deal. The deal was a choice, really. I could give him the names of my drug buddies, or I could attend an Intensive Outpatient Treatment (IOP) for drug abuse.

I chose the treatment. To narc on my friends and fellow dopers would've been self-destructive. I was glad I could make the sacrifice and save my friends.

The IOP was not a success for me. I would get high after each session while I waited for my ride home. The videos they showed my group only served to fuel my attitude about they way we did drugs.

I also attended my first support group meeting while in the program. I don't remember much about it. I know I left feeling certain I did not have a drug or alcohol problem.

I didn't have many run-ins with police. I was usually so paranoid that I worked hard to cover myself and not let very many people know what I was doing.

The rest of my high school years were somewhat uneventful, other than being transferred to the classes for the learning disabled. Eventually, my poor grades and lack of attendance led the school to contact my parents. They seemed to think I needed some special schooling after I was able to convince them my issues were some sort of learning problem. I thought that was a great way to hide the fact that my drug use was the cause.

I eventually flunked out of the special classes. I was only along for the ride and the ride ended up being short. I was expelled on a drug charge. I happened to be serving in-school suspension for missing a couple of days of school, and decided I wanted to get high to help pass the time. So, I fired up right there in the dean's office while the school staff was at lunch.

When they returned, they could obviously smell something unusual. The dean confronted me and told me that my locker would be searched the next day. I was grateful for that because it meant I was going to have enough time to find my locker, get help getting it open and then clean it out.

The next day, they searched the locker and me and found nothing. I probably could've walked out of the trouble that day. But while the search was going on, I had a great idea. All I had to do was admit that I'd been doing the drugs and I could get kicked out of school. My parents wouldn't be able to send me if the school expelled me, so I broke down admitted my crime and was banned from the school property for life.

After being expelled, I started to put together a list of friends who were also dropping out. I figured we would be able to party together and have a great time. The only problem was we didn't have enough money to support our habits. Consequently, it ended up being and "every man for himself" situation, and we soon went our separate ways.

Chapter 3

I was expelled from school in the winter and the weather was cold, as is normal for the Chicago area. I soon discovered the weather was colder than I'd anticipated. My father decided that since I was not in school, was unemployed, and was doing drugs, I should move out of the house.

I agreed to move and thought it would be another opportunity to pursue my carefree lifestyle. I started hiding out in a friend's garage and would sneak around to my house during the day. I didn't last like long that. My friend was opposed to my camping out in his garage, and my father found out I had a house key and promptly confiscated it.

I now had no resources and no connections. Another friend mentioned the Marines were recruiting, so off I went. I figured this was a way to be on my own and would offer the freedom I was seeking.

After a brief interview, the Marine recruiter found out my age and discovered I was about two months too young for the Marines. So, he sent me down the hall to the Navy. The Navy gave me a short written examination. I passed, and was soon on my way to see the world.

I went through the induction, physical, and swearing-in without incident. While I was able to complete everything they asked of me, internally I was a nervous wreck. The night before the exam, I had to have a couple of drinks to get me through.

I got myself sworn-in, and received my first set of orders. I was to report to the Training Base in Illinois.

Well, things at the Great Lakes Naval Training Center were somewhat starker than the TV ads promoted. I was to share a barracks with over one hundred other recruits on the third floor. From the very start, this was a high stress endeavor for me.

We were up every morning by 5:30, and lights were out at 10 p.m.; our days were very busy. Most of the day was spent in classes and learning protocol. We were a staff company, which gave us the privilege of not having to endure the rugged physical workouts some other companies were put through.

At this point, I was losing control because I had no booze to help me stay in line. I experienced my first real hallucination during Boot Camp.

I was in the barracks on a Sunday morning, cleaning my boots and having light conversation with another recruit. It seemed to me that the footlocker I was resting against suddenly landed square on top of me. I then saw a table with ten naked Dreens who were sitting and pointing at me and laughing. They were laughing because I was a weakling and should be bullied.

I was too afraid to say anything. I knew it was not my place to question the Dreens. I did comment to my friend, though. I asked him if he'd ever felt like he'd been run over by a truck. He said no and chuckled. I did not speak of this incident until many years later.

It was very difficult to complete Boot Camp while psychotic. There were many complicated and demanding activities that required one hundred percent effort and commitment. Everything was done in an exacting order on a precise schedule. The things we were learning and doing were taxing. For someone in a psychosis, these things should be impossible.

At one point I volunteered to complete the testing for induction into the Navy SEALS. As I began to complete the orders I was given, I discovered my dislike for intense physical activity was stronger than my desire to be a military hero. So, I declined to complete the testing. I did manage to make our company swim team, though, and was able to help our company make a good showing when we competed against other companies.

There were days when I don't know what kept me going. I know I was driven by fear at times. There was a change taking place inside me, and it was only going to get worse.

Everyday in Boot Camp was an exercise of will. I had developed severe memory problems in high school, and a lot of what I was doing required memory skills. All of my uniforms needed to be stored correctly, worn correctly and this had to be done at the right times. I had to remember insignias for ranks of officers, too. I mean, we had to remember *everything*. And, we were tested on it every day.

I was glad to finally graduate. It was like a big weight was lifted off me. We had a great ceremony with officers and family and friends. I could tell my family was proud of me. As a teenager I hadn't done a lot of things for my parents to be proud of.

My great adventure in the military was about to begin, but first I had more training to complete. I was to go to a Navy Class "A" School. This is where I was sent to learn a skill that was useful. I was somewhat apprehensive about this whole deal, as I was still rather unsure of myself. While I had been so happy to graduate boot camp, I was still somewhat amazed that it had happened.

Right off, I knew I was going to have a hard time at this school. The officer who greeted us and gave us our orientation went through things so quickly I could hardly keep up. There was so much more to this military excursion than what the TV ads had shown.

I was beginning to realize that everything I did somehow impacted someone else. They were doing their best to teach me to be a team player.

While things seemed hard, I did notice I was feeling better and my thinking was clearing some. I related this to being clean and sober. I made my first attempt to stay off the alcohol, as I thought I would need all my resources to complete this training. I managed to stay sober for a couple of days. When I did drink during that time, I drank very little and not very often.

The "A" School was tough. I had a lot of information to learn in just ten weeks. I was being schooled to work aboard aircraft carriers in aircraft maintenance. My responsibility would be to confirm that the planes were ready to fly, and all their parts were in working order.

I didn't do the mechanics of it. I was to complete the paperwork that showed the work had been done. It was an important job, but I thought it was basically work for people with half a working brain cell — like me.

I did okay for the most part. I was able to complete written assignments and passed exams. There was one thing I never did finish, though. I couldn't get my typing skills to twenty words per minute. They kept me an extra week to try to teach me to type, but it was a lost cause.

I finally made nineteen words three times in a row and they passed me.

We had Marines in our school. The Marines were a good bunch, and a lot of fun. I used to go by their barracks and yell, "Hoo-Rah!" They thought it was cool, too, until they found out I was a Navy man. Then, they changed their attitude. I think they thought they had exclusive rights to "Hoo-Rah!"

We had guard duty several times during school. I remember one night in particular. We were guarding some vending machines. I had started out the shift tired, so I was in a foul mood. There were two of us doing this job. After walking around the machines for a while, I lost track of my buddy. I didn't see him for about three hours. I never did find out where he went, and I didn't say anything. It was just strange.

We usually had most of the weekends to ourselves. Some weekends we did guard duty, but that was usually only for four hours. The base had a wonderful set-up. It had a bowling ally, movie theatre, bar and a small store. The officers encouraged us to go into a small city that was close by. But, since there was a bar on the base, I thought I didn't need to leave the base.

The rest of my training was mostly uneventful. Although at one morning assembly, my psychosis almost got out. I was at attention and chewing on my cheek. My instructor asked me to spit out my gum, and I informed him I didn't have any gum. I got yelled at for a while after that. I'm not sure exactly what he said, but it seemed important.

When he finished, he turned and went to the front of the assembly and noticed me chewing again. I got the same treatment with an added deep inspection of my mouth for gum. I finally convinced him that I had no gum, and he convinced me to stop chewing on the inside of my cheek.

I had to travel to another base to finish training. This would be "on the job training," just like in real life. I had regular working hours, a supervisor, and jobs to complete. I was feeling one hundred percent better. I think this was because I hadn't been drinking much and had stayed off the marijuana. I was starting to believe I could handle this Navy stuff after all.

I would show up to work on time. I was in uniform, high and tight. I was actually feeling happy.

About two days into the training, I decided the status board for the maintenance of aircraft was disorganized. I redesigned the board and the way things were posted on it. I was thinking what a wonderful job I'd done about the same time my senior officer was thinking that someone had come into his world and done something that wasn't right.

Reorganized or no, he let me know the board needed to be back the way it had been immediately. This was not easy, because I'd thrown away the original cards. To fix this, I had to retype the notes and place them where they'd been before. This was after I'd pointed out how much better my way looked and how much more organized it was.

I was actually doing better and was getting things done in order. I was focused on not drinking, again, and as a result, was drinking much less.

I would go visit my parents when I had the time. I got to see some of my high school friends and was making a comeback with those relationships. I was back on my game and off to the races, again.

Some time later, it came to the attention of my superiors that I'd been drinking more frequently and was missing some of my training. This, of course, was entirely unacceptable. I was brought in for a sit-down with the staff officers.

During this session, my drinking habits were the focus of this conversation. I was sunk. I think I'm the only sailor who was not allowed on ships. I was inwardly glad to be landlocked. This meant less stress and more opportunity to continue with my pursuit of alcoholic beverages.

The fun and games I was planning came to an abrupt halt when it was decided I needed to be transferred to a station more suited for someone with my lack of respect for authority. I was given a choice of assignments, and then told which choice to make. Just like that, I was transferred.

I was sent to a base in Louisiana, just a little way from New Orleans. Man, Mardi Gras. What luck for a guy like me who likes to party. I thought this was going to be great. I was really looking forward to it. For the life of me, I can't figure out why they thought this was the best place to send me.

I decided to hitchhike to the base and try to save money for beer. The hitch hiking was okay, but I was almost late. I was able to make it to the base with about five minutes to spare.

Once I arrived, things got under way quickly. I was given a room assignment, shown the laundry, and the mess hall was pointed out to me. The base was pretty big. It had all the usual facilities, along with a golf course, a theatre, and an enlisted men's club. I found the enlisted men's club very interesting. Even though I was seventeen years old, I could get served there, at least for a while.

I opted to room in the old barracks. There were fewer occupants and there was a beer machine. Beer was only a fifty-cents and it was always ice cold, so the beer machine tended to empty out rather quickly. Besides, the old barracks were pretty far away from any busy areas. This made partying easier and less noticeable.

I thought I was going to do well here. My spirits were good, and I was going to make a serious attempt to get things to come out right. I was able to get settled in and began to try to make friends.

After about a week, I started having trouble getting to work on time. I was late and, sometimes, my uniform was not up to par. I tended to let my hair get too long, too, and now my hygiene was worse.

It seemed my pay went pretty quickly and a few days after payday I was always short on money. I never could figure that out. I would get paid and go get drunk. Then it always seemed like about three days later I was broke.

It was a good thing the rent was paid and the mess hall didn't charge for meals most times. There were a couple of times I was charged at the mess hall when I either showed up late or was out of uniform. If I'd had to pay for those things on a regular basis, I would've been in trouble.

I remember one night when the evil spirits were more active than usual. I was on my way back to my room after spending some time in the enlisted men's club. Of course, I was a little drunk, as was normal. The vampires were really trying to get me. They chased me all the way across the base. I don't know why they didn't chase me into my room. When I made it to the barracks, they stayed outside.

When I got to the hallway where my room was, I started feeling better. I got on my flying throne and was zipping around the barracks hallways. I had to fight Thor and Odin because they thought I was out of line and shouldn't have such privileges as a flying throne. After all, I was only a mortal. I guess they didn't know much about me.

I don't know how long I spent beating those two guys up. I showed them they couldn't control me. I also made it clear that they were not to interfere with my activities. They never bothered with me again.

When I woke up, I knew it was late. I didn't even try to make it to work on time. I figured if there was a war they'd know where to find me.

It was at about this time I was excluded from drinking in the enlisted men's club. I had to take my drinking off the base. I found that most bartenders accepted my military identification as legitimate. That made getting alcohol easy, and somewhat legal.

I had a bad habit of going into New Orleans. I liked the French Quarter, and would drink heavily there. Doing this would always end with me out of money, and no way to make the twenty-mile trip back to the base.

The first time this happened, I actually walked all night and made it to work on time. But that was the only time I made it back like that.

By the time the Navy caught up with me, I had seven unauthorized absences charged to me, and was detained and held for a Captain's Mass. At the Mass, I was found guilty of unauthorized absences and given ninety days in the Brig.

The Captain's Mass was held up by the fact that I was out of uniform and needed a hair cut. The Base Commander was completely unhappy with my performance. There had been other runs-ins with him, and I think those things were fresh in his memory.

There was a Navy lawyer that seemed to understand something was wrong with me and I think that was why I received such a light sentence. I could've really been in serious trouble if I'd received the maximum.

I was pretty sick. I was hallucinating and wasn't able to think clearly. I'd had my first serious bouts with hallucinations just before this arrest.

I remember a period of time when I thought the air was fire. It was a clear fire that couldn't be seen, but there was a burning sensation that accompanied it. It seemed to me that I could smell the burning flesh of those around me. I had some serious problems.

There was one day when it was cold out and I'd been wandering around the French Quarter for some time. I felt tired and cold and sat down on a street curb to rest. I remember thinking that I should create a sun. Not a big sun, just one large enough to help me warm up.

I did that, and started to feel quite warm there under my sun. I was enjoying myself when along came a giant silhouette of a man. He stole my silver sun and ran away with it. I was disappointed, and angry.

I would walk for endless spells. I have no idea how much of New Orleans I walked through. I do remember that as I walked, the earth and all of reality would vanish behind me. As I stepped forward, reality would only be in front of me, never behind. Behind me, there was only nothing.

I had what I still believe to be the most amazing hallucination at about this same time. Late one night, as I walked back to the base, I happened to pass a dry cleaning store. As I looked in the big front window, I spied a Coke machine. In I went, put the money in the machine and got my Coke.

It was at that time the clerk came out and asked me how I'd gotten in, as the store was closed. I told him I came in through the door. He replied that the door was locked. I didn't think too much of it as I stepped atop a chair near the window, and then stepped out through the window and onto the street. I did this without breaking the window.

I have absolutely no idea what actually took place. My sick brain tells me I walked through a locked door and then out through a window.

After the trial, I was taken to the Brig via Paddy Wagon. I remember thinking this was no way to treat someone as good as I was. After all, I'd created the world and people should be thanking me.

When they started completing my entry into the Brig, they found I had no uniforms. I needed uniforms to complete my sentence. One of the nice officers went out and purchased uniforms for me and brought them back. One of my fellow convicts stenciled my name and number onto them for me. I was starting to feel like I was being treated better.

The next morning, I slept in. When the turnkey came to wake me, I foiled his vision and made myself to appear to be crucified on a cross. I'm not sure what he saw, but he left me alone that day. It may have been that I was naked. When one is crucified, it is done without clothing.

I fell into the routine well enough. I was up early for the physical workout every morning. After that, we had really good meals at the Mess Hall, and then we spent the day working on various projects. I was rotated around pretty quickly.

I was assigned to prepare and paint a wall in the rear of the lock up where we were incarcerated. I was to take off the old paint and prepare the wall for new paint. My method of cleaning the wall was to chip the paint with a metal tool.

I was told to scrape the paint, but chipping was faster. Chipping left craters in the brick. I found out there was no way to smooth the wall once it was chipped like that. I also found out they would transfer me if I continued to attempt to destroy the wall.

Something more insidious was occurring at this time. I found that I started to have lapses in conscious thought. I would suddenly become aware that I was sitting and staring into space. I tried to stop myself, but there was nothing I could do. It started happening over and over.

I do remember that I realized I had been doing this for some time, but had not been aware of it. The painful part of it was that no matter how hard I tried to pay attention, I would still have these lapses. I called it "spacing out."

After a brief meeting with the Captain, who was in charge of the Brig, he told me I needed to finish my sentence with good behavior or I'd have to stay longer.

I was able to hold myself together long enough to finish my time and then be transferred to my regular duty station. I was able to get back there, but I was two days late and out of uniform when I arrived.

When I got back, I opted to stay in the old barracks again. I wanted as little contact with others as I could manage. By this time, I was aware I had problems. I would lose things and couldn't for the life of me figure things out.

The first thing I did when I arrived was to get squared away and find a party. I found a party, but it wasn't much fun. Somehow, I hooked up with some locals and began my usual routine of getting loaded. I'm not sure exactly what I did. I remember making a very big fellow angry, though, and wound up in a fight. I got hurt and had to call 911 for help. When the ambulance arrived, I asked them to take me to the base hospital. The base hospital then transferred me to the county hospital for treatment.

Once at the hospital, I was examined and began to behave somewhat bizarrely. I remember hearing a baby cry and my telling the ER team that it was my child. I don't remember much other than those couple of things. I do remember seeing white. It's hard to explain. When I would "space out," I could see white. It was as if I was staring at a bright light. This would happen again some years later.

I don't know what I was treated for at the hospital. I remember being there for a few days. While I was there, it was suggested I go to Alcoholics Anonymous. I agreed to go because it was a good way to get off the hospital ward.

At the meeting I was greeted warmly. I was also given a marble and some instructions. The instructions were to keep the marble with me. If I thought I was going to drink, I needed to throw the marble as far as I could because I'd lost my marbles.

After the meeting, I went outside and threw the marble as far as I could. It seemed to be what I wanted to do. I didn't drink right then, but I had lost my marbles.

Eventually the county hospital doctor transferred me to a psychiatric unit in another hospital. By this time, I was out of it. I was telling the staff and other patients I was Jesus Christ. For a couple of days, I wouldn't speak to anyone unless they addressed me as Jesus or God Almighty. There were a couple of days I didn't speak to anyone.

I was also started on psychiatric medication at this time. I remember receiving injections of Thorazine. I also remember that it had no effect on me whatsoever. It didn't slow me down one bit. I didn't sleep for the first couple of days.

I also had some other first experiences. It was the first time I was in restraints. I remember being restrained, but I don't remember what for. It seemed to me I had asked what it was like to be in restraints, so I was put in restraints. I also got loose, and was able to move about seclusion freely.

There was a moment when they should've let me use the restroom. When they didn't respond to my request to use the restroom, I went in a garbage can. I felt sorry for the guy who had to clean that up. I also refused to tell them how I got out of restraints. That was a trade secret.

I was given a lot of tests, x-rays, and whatever else they wanted. I remember thinking I needed to pass these tests, even though the doc said they weren't that kind of tests. I think I must've failed because they kept me for a couple of weeks and then transferred me to a military hospital psychiatric ward.

This was an experience that would form my lifestyle for the next eleven years. It was here that I learned to be a patient. I must say, I was not a model patient, though.

I was started on Lithium and told I had Manic Depression. I also slept for a couple of days upon arrival. This seemed like a safe haven for me. I was getting enough rest and food, and started to feel better.

For the next decade, anytime I started to feel better it meant I was ready to party, again.

The doctors at the hospital were competent and caring, but I think they most often felt at a loss for what do with us. There was no real treatment. They would give me tranquilizers and hope I would calm down. For the most part I did, but I had a lot of fun, too.

I thought that since they didn't really treat me, it was my duty to go ahead and have fun anyway. I tried smuggling in beer. I would get all-day passes and give a promise to not drink, and I would come back pretty lit up.

I remember not being able to think very well during this time. It seemed I focused a lot of energy on what others were doing and how I could bother them. It was a lot of fun most times. I didn't usually end up in a fight or anything too terrible. I did really bother some of the other patients, though. They would pursue their various interests, and I would try their tolerance and patience.

I remember signing a legal document while I was there. It was some sort of statement that released the Navy of any responsibility for my condition. Even though I believe the stress in the service started my psychosis, this document was cause for them to refuse my future attempts to collect a service connected disability claim.

I am grateful for the opportunity to work and feel normal today. So, maybe it's a good thing I didn't get the disability pension after all.

Chapter 4

To make a long story short, I was discharged from the Navy soon after my release from the military hospital. My adventure home started right off with me being victimized. I had hitchhiked to the Navy base in Louisiana after OJT, and I thought I could save money by hitching back to my parents' place in Indiana. Well, that was a good idea, but not the way things went.

I started out well enough, with a sea bag full of clothes, a pocket full of severance pay, and an ounce of marijuana. I was really planning on having fun.

I got picked up right away. These two nice-looking fellows offered to give me a ride through to Mobile, Alabama. I felt I was off to a good start.

About a half hour into the ride, the driver said he wanted to stop to take a break. I thought that was a good idea and agreed. I needed a break myself.

He pulled off the main highway and drove down a dirt track of a road. It seemed our break was going to be behind some bushes. As he stopped the car, he leaned over the seat from the front and shoved a gun in my face.

He ordered me out of the car, told me to give them what they wanted and I'd be all right.

I got out of the car all right, and did what they ordered. I was told to strip. So, I stripped. I was left with a t-shirt and no pride. As they made sure they had all of my stuff, they also told me to take off running. As I started to run, one of them started shooting at me, or in my general direction. I didn't hesitate; I ran as fast as I could.

I ended up running into a swampy area that was full of poison oak and some sort of poisonous thistle. Being mostly naked, I cut my feet and legs up pretty badly. Even so, I was happy that I'd gotten away and the highwaymen didn't pursue me. I thought I'd hide in the marsh for a while and then make an attempt to get help.

Just as I was about to come out of hiding, I heard some laughter and saw some boys swimming in a small pond. I was afraid. I was half naked and these kids were just 150 feet from my hiding place. I worried that if someone saw me there, they might not believe my story and think I had bad intentions. So, I stayed hidden until they left and I could come out safely.

After that, I began to try to make my way back to the road. I was able to pick up my boots; they'd left them behind. I put them on and then took off my t-shirt and made a makeshift cover for my privates that ended up looking like a big diaper. I had this mental image of "Baby Huey".

As I made my way to the road, I saw a man changing a flat tire on his car. I thought this was a Godsend. I hoped the man would help me. I'm not sure exactly what kind of help I thought I needed, though.

Instead of trying to get close to him, I called from a distance. I didn't want to spook him. Luckily, I found a good person that afternoon. This kind stranger helped me out with a pair of pants, a t-shirt and a brand new pair of underwear. He also gave me a lift to the nearest hospital so I could get my feet and legs treated. I had poison oak, and who knows what else from my knees down on both legs. I was also all scratched up and bleeding.

The good Samaritan dropped me off at the hospital and bid me farewell. I was glad to be able to get some treatment for my legs. They really looked bad. Fortunately, they looked worse than they were. I washed well, and then the police wanted me to look at some mug shots and to try to identify the two guys who had held me up.

I'm afraid I wasn't much use. I was psychotic and schizophrenic and fresh out of a trauma. I wasn't able to do much at all.

I contacted my family in Northwestern Indiana and my father wired me enough money for a bus ticket home. The bus ride was uneventful and very long. I was entertaining to the other passengers, though. It seemed I was able to be funny and act without inhibitions.

Once I arrived home, it was easy for my family to see I was somehow different than when I left. They weren't sure if the difference was good or bad. I soon made my condition obvious, as my mental illness was now completely out of control.

I was not able to carry on normal conversation. The content of my dialogue was often inflammatory and controversial. I would say things like, "I'm the third greatest power in the universe." Or, as I walked in the woods with my younger brother I asked, "Have you ever been killed by an axe murderer?"

I made these statements and I didn't think my comments were unusual. It was impossible for me to see I was sick. My disease had snuck up on me and taken control.

My mother was educated, somewhat, on this whole mental illness thing. This was not the first time she'd been exposed to it. She could recognize symptoms and knew I was in trouble long before I did. She was able to act on her knowledge and have me admitted to a psychiatric unit in a hospital.

This was not my first visit to such a place. Over the next eight years, I would make many visits to places like this. Sometimes, I was glad to return, because this seemed to be the only safe place for me.

At first I was reluctant to enter. I didn't think I needed to be there. I was still blind to the fact that I was ill. The only recourse for my family and the doctors was to have me involuntarily committed. So, I was committed for a ninety-day inpatient stay.

The first thing the doctor did was order some tranquilizers. Boy, I thought that sounded good. I could get high, and I would be fine. I soon realized these tranquilizers didn't make me high. They seemed rather strong, though, and made me really sleepy.

For the most part, I was agreeable to treatment. I tried to catch on and follow the rules. It's hard to follow rules that don't seem to make sense or seem to be just a rule without reason. My Navy training came in useful and I seemed able to follow the rules somewhat, with only minor difficulty.

The medications they gave me began to change me. I was tired all the time, and they wouldn't let me sleep. I learned to find out-of-the-way places so I could sleep. The nurses seemed intent on keeping me awake, but I just couldn't do it.

It also really messed up my appetite. When I was admitted to the hospital I weighed in at 165 pounds. After ninety days, my weight was around 220 pounds. I learned that taking medications had a high price. They kept me from completely losing control, but I had to suffer in other ways.

Because this was an involuntary commitment, I had to stay, like it or not. I really didn't have much in the way of thoughts during this time. I can remember that I spent long hours sitting and staring into space.

There was a realization setting in that would form my attitude and behaviors for years to come. I realized that my life was gone. I had mental illness, and the best I could hope for was charity. I realized I wouldn't be able to work or maintain any kind of independence. This hopelessness would be the guiding factor in my life for the next decade.

For years, I spent my time living in poor neighborhoods and was in and out of the psychiatric hospital. My drinking and drugging continued unabated. Generally, I felt I had no direction or purpose. These were years when I spiraled ever lower. I was without hope to achieve my dreams, and had no motivation to try.

After release from that first hospitalization, I moved into a halfway house for persons with mental illness. It was a program with good and bad points. The staff there genuinely cared for the residents, and tried to make a difference. I spent eighteen months there.

The halfway house had rules to follow that helped reintegrate us into the community. The programs were well intentioned, but to those of us without hope they held no real promise.

I had problems there that were made worse by my continued drinking and drug use. I also realized I felt out of place, even with the other residents. I'm not sure where that feeling came from. I think it may be that I had no feelings at all. The only time I ever really felt anything was when I was under the influence.

One program at the house was to help residents find employment. I was sent out in the morning to visit businesses and complete applications for employment. My idea of completing this was to go to a number of businesses and get a business card or a matchbook with the company information on it, then spend the rest of the day at the city park sleeping under a tree.

I eventually was enrolled in a sheltered workshop program. I made little money there and felt I didn't fit in. I think most of the other employees were somehow disadvantaged, but not mentally ill, so I felt like an outsider.

My feelings about working there were negative. There were many days when I skipped work and stayed in bed all day. My depression and lack of enthusiasm toward my life was punctuated by binges of total oblivion brought on by heavy drinking.

I did manage to have one good accomplishment while in the program. I was able to get my GED. This was the first accomplishment I'd had in a long while, and it felt good. I remember taking the pre-test and passing. I then paid my fee for the regular test and returned a few days later to take the exam.

I sat to finish the test, and worked hard on it. I was almost finished when I got up to take a smoke break. Upon my return, I couldn't find my desk with my test, so I approached the instructor and found she had picked up it up while I was smoking. She told me that once I got up, I could not return to complete the test. It had something to do with eliminating cheating.

Well, she graded my incomplete test and informed I'd passed. If I'd known it was so easy, I would've taken it years ago.

The next eight years I drifted from the neighborhood to inpatient treatment to my parent's house. My parents are good people. Through the many years of my struggles, my family always did their best to be supportive and do the right thing. Sometimes, the right thing meant that I had to leave. My drinking continued, and my behavior was not conducive to community living.

I only had a few friends, and we were brought together by our common problems. There was no way for us to develop long term relationships. Most of us were in and out of the hospital so much that we were seldom around.

My feelings about my life were becoming worse at this point. As I grew older, I also grew more hopeless. I felt more than ever that I wouldn't succeed or have the things in life I'd always wanted.

There were some confusing issues I was struggling to deal with. These things seem to me to be double-edged.

As I wandered aimlessly through life, I had become involved with a support group that I enjoyed. There were some very good people there who were trying to help me stay sober. Those people helped to make my life tolerable, and somewhat easier. At the same time, I was continuing with the attitude of hopelessness; it had become part of me.

It's difficult to understand that on one hand I was serious about getting well, and at the same time I did things that were directly opposed to those ideas. I find it baffling to this day. Eventually, my efforts at getting well would pay off, but that wouldn't happen until years later.

At this time in my life, I was sinking into my worst nightmare.

Chapter 5

It was during this time that I made my first serious attempt at suicide. I decided my life here on earth was pointless and going nowhere. The thought of dying became attractive in the sense that this life would be over, and I could go on into eternity and start fresh. I acted on that thinking, and took an intentional overdose.

My roommate found me, and could tell I was having problems. At some point, I'd fallen down and seriously cut my face and it was bleeding pretty badly. Plus, the drugs were having such a strong effect on me that I couldn't talk. My roommate thought I was drunk at first, but soon realized it was something more serious and called for an ambulance.

Because of the large number of pills I'd taken, I was forced to drink this awful black stuff and they shoved a tube down my throat to pump my stomach. That was all I remember. Everything went black. It was total darkness.

In the moment before I woke up, I thought I was in the presence of angels. I don't really recall much more than seeing figures shining with an intense white light.

As I opened my eyes, I saw my parents and a nurse. I remember thinking that I'd fouled things up because I was still alive. I then learned that I'd been in a drug-induced coma for four days, and that I had come within minutes of dying.

After a few days, my parents decided I could move back home. I could stay there if I could follow the usual conditions of being alcohol and drug free. They didn't really push me to get a job, but I did anyway. I found work, bought a small truck and felt pretty good for a change.

I started to really apply myself and was making progress. But soon, I started smoking marijuana again, and that changed my attitude. Within a few days, I was back to feeling empty and hopeless and tried another intentional drug overdose.

This time my father found me, and called an ambulance. I remember little about what happened next. I do remember drinking that black stuff again, and I fought with the paramedics when they tried to shove a tube down my throat. Then everything was black, and quiet, and empty. I had entered another coma, and stayed there for a few days.

I think I should include a factor I believe contributed to my suicide attempts. The reason I want to add this is I believe it is relevant to my suicidal ideations.

Three months before my first suicide attempt, I'd been prescribed an antidepressant. I complained of sleep difficulties to my psychiatrist and he prescribed this antidepressant to help me sleep. I believe that antidepressants had a significant role in my second attempt, as well.

The reason I make this statement is that prior to the antidepressant medication, I had no problems with suicidal thoughts or ideations. Since that second attempt, I haven't been on any antidepressants and have not had further suicidal tendencies.

At this point, my parents were convinced I couldn't successfully live at home. My behavior had certainly proven I was out of control. They made it clear I could not move back in with them. So, I was forced to return to the halfway house I'd been in during my original treatment. The only problem was, they didn't have space for me.

The director of the program said that if I could manage myself in the community for one year with no drug or alcohol abuse and no suicide attempts, I'd be eligible to return to their program.

I remember thinking, *If I could do all of that for one year, then I wouldn't need that program.* As I was investigating this possibility, I was inpatient at my usual hospital. I was informed that after I was discharged this time, if I returned, I would be committed to a state hospital for one year.

As of today, I have not been in an inpatient setting as a patient for seventeen years. But, at this point in my life, things got worse; more so than I ever thought possible.

I was still getting high and drinking, and the drugs and alcohol were still making me feel the way I wanted to feel. By this point, I didn't want to feel anything; I just wanted to feel high. I didn't have much in the way of my own feelings. I spent my time feeling drugs and whatever I could get to alter my mind.

I did manage to find a small efficiency apartment that I could afford with my disability money. I was able to get a discount on the deposit and I moved in. My parents helped me move my belongings. I remember my father being supportive and offering his guidance on getting stable and focusing on work.

My mother was not too optimistic about my chances. She didn't know what to do for me. My situation was beyond her control. I know she prayed for me. She'd been praying for me for a long time.

I managed to land a job cleaning a department store. I was getting to work on time and was performing in an acceptable fashion. Then, I started to feel it was time for change and decided I was going on an adventure.

I decided to sell my belongings and get my deposit back. I did just that and bought a bus ticket. I wanted a bus ticket for the west coast, but I only had enough for a ticket to Denver.

Soon, I was on the road with no responsibilities or anyone to answer to. For someone as sick as I was, this was a bad place to be.

I kept little in the way of clothes, and brought a little food with me so I wouldn't have to spend money to eat. I wasn't thinking straight, and was making one bad decision after another.

The really sad part about all of this was I couldn't see the judgments were bad and the decisions were unhealthy. I can only see the mistakes in retrospect, though. It is my belief that a person in psychosis cannot recognize the illness in that state. It is only after, and rarely before, the onset that one can see the disease manifest in themselves.

What had been so obvious to my family and friends for years was only now starting to take shape in my mind. It would still be years before I came out of this state of not seeing, and the worst of it was still to come.

As I left on the bus to Denver, I felt some trepidation about my immediate future, but I decided that this was the right thing to do. A large part of my attitude still centered on my mental picture of my life. I thought my life was just going to be staying on medication and staying out of the hospital. With these thoughts governing my behavior, getting up and leaving town didn't seem at all unusual. So I was off and down the road.

I met some nice people on the bus and found I could be quite entertaining. In so doing, I concocted a story about how I was on my way to Los Angeles to become a famous comedian.

In my years as a person living with schizophrenia, I had become adept at making up lies about my past and future. I didn't want anyone to know I had to have treatment and hospitalizations, or that I took medications. I felt I was somehow worth less than others and if they knew this about me they would treat me poorly.

I knew I was right in this belief. In the few times when I revealed these startling facts about myself, I'd been ridiculed and criticized. Sometimes, I felt some of the mental health workers viewed me as less than, too, instead of equal but sick.

The bus arrived in Denver and I disembarked. I didn't really have a plan. I wanted to make it to California, but I was broke. I saw some other broke people panhandling and it seemed to work. So, I started panhandling.

I was actually doing pretty well at it. I was getting some donations and was able to use my newfound charm to convince others I was a worthy cause. I was accumulating money, but it was slow going and the donations were usually small.

I did have a nice leather jacket I'd brought with me and was able to sell it for $100. Now, I had enough for a ticket to Las Vegas. It was good I came up with the money because the police had decided I needed to go to another state and bother somebody else for a while.

I only had enough money to get to Vegas and buy a couple of meals. I thought I'd be okay. I hadn't been drinking for a couple of months and felt I'd be able to stay sober. I didn't have enough money to buy drugs, so I felt good about staying clean. I'd even stopped taking the Antibuse I had left. *Why not?* I thought. *I'm not going to drink anyway.* I was still charming people on the bus and felt pretty good.

When I got off the bus in Las Vegas, the first thing I saw was a sign that read "Cold Beer One Cent Per Glass". The next thing I did was buy two rolls of pennies. I figured one hundred glasses of beer would be a good start to my stay in Vegas. There was a little voice in the back of my head that urged me to call AA instead of going to the bar, but the demon alcohol won out again.

During the next couple of days, I drank heavily and I don't remember much. I'm sure I must've made a nuisance of myself. In any case, I was broke again. I found out Las Vegas is the worst place to be homeless. I was surrounded by billions of dollars and didn't have enough money for a cheeseburger.

I did learn how to get to soup kitchens and other charities for the homeless. Some nights, I'd go to a mission and listen to a sermon so I could get the free meal afterwards. I also learned about the Salvation Army. It was there I received a card good for food and lodging, but I lost it and never did go back.

I can remember sleeping on the ground after having walked to the point of exhaustion. At those times, I would lie down and sleep anywhere I could. Sometimes, it would be on the sidewalk or any empty lot. One afternoon, I was so tired that I lay down on the floor of a convenient store behind a pop machine and slept there until I was discovered and kicked out.

Things in Vegas were not going well for me. I didn't try to look up AA, although I probably should've done that. I was a mess and without recourse to remedy my situation. I was starting to believe I was having some kind of problem that was interfering with successfully living in the world.

Somewhere in my lizard brain, the thought of despair was growing in shape and strength. For some time, the extent of my thinking had focused on how I made some bad choices. There were many times when my problems should've caused me to change my habits and behavior. My solution was always to drink. As long as I could feel the effects of alcohol and drugs, I didn't need to feel anything else. It was my way of feeling and thinking *and* my ball and chain.

I don't remember exactly how it happened, but I finally hooked up with some other hopeless folks. I must admit they were pretty wealthy. They had a thirty-year-old car with no brakes. But hey, that was considerably more than I had. They also didn't mind me hanging around. I drank the way they did and wasn't afraid to approach people to panhandle money.

I had a little break, though. I decided to call home to let my family know I was still alive. This call was a small comfort to them. During the course of our conversation, I realized my disability checks had kept coming in. I asked my parents to wire me the money. My father was somewhat reluctant to do this, but I convinced him the money would help my situation.

Once the money was wired, I left for San Francisco with my new buddies in their beat up old car with no brakes. It was quite a drive through the mountains. Going up was a piece of cake. Coming down was something else entirely. We did manage to cross the Rockies without incident.

Once we arrived in San Francisco, we located soup kitchens and the Plasma Alliance donation centers. I would continue to donate for the next several years, as it became my chief source of income for buying cigarettes. There were some times when it was revenue for booze, also.

I think being homeless in California was too easy. There were plenty of soup kitchens and missions with free overnight stays. I never really experienced severe homelessness. In the not so distant future, though, I certainly would.

We were able to keep enough gas in the old car to keep it moving so we weren't ticketed for vagrancy. The car was a home away from home. We used it as a mobile hotel and would take turns sleeping in the backseat, as the front seat was not comfortable for sleeping.

I was also able to contact my father again and convinced him to send more money from my check. This money was coming in handy and it made me a source of income for the group. This meant they would let me keep hanging around. I think if I hadn't had that money, they would've run me off.

We did leave San Francisco, but I would return some weeks later. It would be during that time I that would experience my darkest hours.

As I stayed with that crew, my drinking continued unabated, and my drug use went hand in hand with my drinking. I was still enjoying the effects of the drink and the drugs. As long as it was enjoyable and fun, I wasn't able to let it go.

How could I still be having fun? I'd left everything I owned. I'd abandoned everyone I knew. The drink still felt good. I could relax and forget my problems. My drug use was something I viewed more as a coping tool than an addiction. Besides, with my drug use, I had always stuck to pot, and pot wasn't addictive. Even though I spent years stealing money from everyone I knew to buy more pot, I thought it wasn't addictive. Of course, in my mind, it wasn't.

After a short time, we decided to drive to Reno to gamble. It was our intention to try to make some money. We thought we might be able to win enough to buy gas for the car, as well as food and lodging for ourselves. We arrived in Reno with the car on empty and our pockets near exhausted.

Chapter 6

We did manage to win enough to support ourselves for several days. We continued to sleep in the car. When it was time to win money for food or gas, we would clean up in a gas station restroom and visit the casinos.

During this time in the casinos, I learned about free drinks. If I played at the slot machines, the waitresses would come around every so often and bring free drinks as I played. So, I developed a way to play as slow as humanely possible, extending the period of time where I could get free beer.

This was working out nicely. I was winning enough to buy food and had free booze. I was starting to like this place.

For some unknown or not remembered reason, we decided to leave Reno and move our little operation to Las Vegas. It was in Vegas that things really took a turn for the worse. This was, for me, my rapid descent into hell.

Of course I was drinking as much as I could, and I started having trouble following through on our system of free drinks and slot money for meals. I don't remember exactly how I did it, but I managed to lose all the money we had left.

My traveling companions were somewhat angry, and ready to strangle me. But, I convinced them that I could have more money wired from home, so they spared me. I am serious when I say they probably would've have killed me over this.

We decided to head to Sacramento to hang out in missions and soup kitchens until I could get the money wired to me. Our plans changed abruptly when we arrived.

We started out looking to kill some time and wait for the money. What we did was end up becoming buddy-buddy with some locals who had a nice spot by the river. It was here that we that we set up a new system of survival. And yet, I was only a few days from hell.

We had a system of rotation. Some days we donated plasma, other days we took turns in soup kitchens. There was one fellow there who had a cash job. He would deliver flyers door to door and get paid at the end of the day. He spent the money on cigarettes and beer. Most of the time, we had enough free food, and this man's generosity kept our vices well supplied.

It was summer, and we were living on the banks of a river. We did a lot of swimming and drinking. We did a lot of sunbathing and drinking. When we didn't drink, we smoked and did whatever else we could find.

This is where I did LSD for the first time. I must say, I wasn't impressed. I didn't feel much of anything. I told the guy who tried to collect money from us for the LSD to take a flying leap. I guess he must've, because he left and I never saw him again.

I don't know whose property we were squatting on, but no one ever came to kick us out. So, we stayed. I don't remember for how long, but it was weeks, I'm sure.

We met some very interesting people camping out there. There were mainly lots of dopers and other sordid individuals. On one occasion, someone ticked off this biker crew. I'm sure they won't be doing that again.

By now, our little party was coming to end. We were getting dissatisfied with each other, and most of our conversations ended in arguments. We seldom went for more than a few hours with out an animated disagreement.

At this point, I managed to land a job from an older couple. It was my main job to help them take care of their property. I mowed grass, roofed their garage and basically helped them keep their property up and looking nice. I wanted to stay on and keep working there, but they wanted me to leave. I must have done something, but I don't recall what that may have been.

I was clearly psychotic at this time. I can only remember thoughts that were driven by fear. I don't think I was hallucinating, but it's hard to remember. What has impressed itself on my memory is that at this time, nothing seemed to work out.

After I left the old folks, I headed back to Sacramento. I managed to find the same crew of guys, but we only lasted a couple of days together. When we split up and went our separate ways, I was alone again. Hell was only hours from me now, but I didn't see it.

So, here I am. I've got a little money and no comrades, as we've now broken our alliance. I'm starting to feel a little out of sorts, and I don't know where to go exactly.

I suddenly have the urge to go to San Francisco. My thinking is that maybe I can find work there. I knew there must be more soup kitchens there than in Sacramento.

I took most of the money I had then and bought a bus ticket to the Bay City. I knew I could survive better there. I felt like I was making progress and needed to keep all of this in perspective.

Here I am with no money, no friends, my family a long distance away, and I've not been on my meds for a few months. I'm saying I'm feeling better and I feel like I'm making progress, but in reality I was in worse shape than I knew. I was going to find pain in a form I hadn't experienced before or since.

I don't remember the bus ride to San Francisco. I vaguely remember buying the ticket and getting on the bus. I have only the foggiest memory of being on the bus. I think I must have been drunk and in a blackout.

I do know that upon my arrival I left the bus station and walked in the wrong direction. I walked for several hours before it dawned on me that I needed to turn around.

I went to a phone booth and called a cab, and spent the rest of my money on a ride back downtown. The bus station was only a few blocks from downtown, but my walking took me a long way from there.

Something happened inside of my brain. It was as if someone had thrown a switch. I no longer felt confident or energetic. Now I felt confused and lost. The world had gone from tolerable to darkness and despair.

I did my best to keep my spirits up, and I tried to get a better attitude. All of my efforts were to no avail. I had sunk as deep as one can go short of death, and death began to have a strong appeal.

I managed to find a soup kitchen and got some food. I was bewildered. I remember wondering why I couldn't manage myself or take the necessary actions to find shelter and food.

I fell into a pattern of walking and panhandling. I also engaged in less glamorous activity to get food and some shelter, if only for a little while. I felt lost, and for the most part I *was* lost.

I started having a lot of problems remembering addresses for the soup kitchens and I wasn't able to communicate to others that I needed help. It seemed every avenue of opportunity was blocked for me.

I would get very tired from walking for hours. Every once in a while, the police would stop me. Sometimes, I'd be sitting in a place where I shouldn't have been. Or maybe I'd slumped down from exhaustion.

The police would check our identification and let us go if we had no warrants. Since I had no warrants, they always let me go on. I think they knew something was wrong with me, but they didn't have the resources to deal with my type of problem.

It came to a point where all of my perceptions contained pain. It was painful to think. It was painful to try to not think. I could no longer blot out the pain with alcohol. I was getting to the point where I could hardly hold myself together enough to panhandle for money.

My pattern consisted of walking for hours and hours and then finally dropping down into a deep sleep. When I woke up, I would repeat the cycle. This happened over and over. I don't know how many days or weeks I went on like this. It was long enough to wear out one pair of shoes and grow a full beard. I was malnourished and psychotic and I was only getting worse.

In one instance I remember a nice fellow helped me out with some food and shelter for a couple of days. But I think I was so sick that he asked me to move on.

I had some run-ins with local gangs, too, but they usually showed pity on me. I think they could tell I had other problems. Most of the people I met seemed to know I was having issues, even though they weren't sure what the problem was.

The memories I have of those times are single instances lying about like broken toys in an old and deserted attic. The one thread all of those things have in common is that they all are painful in some way. Some memories are painful to remember and others are too painful to forget.

One of these is my late night walk in Golden Gate Park. I was so hungry that I ate petals from flowers and leaves from trees. I remember that night more because of the food I found.

As I walked in my usual stooped over gait, I spied a brown lunch sack on the ground. I went over to it and picked it up and looked inside. To my surprise and joy there were two sandwiches inside the bag. I remember a brief thought about the sandwiches being spoiled, but my hunger overcame my caution, and I ate both sandwiches. I think that was the only food I'd had for at least one twenty-four period.

One night, after an extremely long walk, I stumbled across a fellow in need of help. I found him face down in the gutter. He was unconscious, and I felt he was vulnerable. I thought I should probably get his wallet and take his money. After all, he wouldn't notice.

I was suddenly gripped by the fear of getting caught. I thought about what would happen if someone saw me. So, I walked past him. As I left, I thought of it again, and I ended up walking around the block three times, but could never bring myself to rob him.

Later, as the hunger pains started again, taking his money seemed to be a good idea. Lucky for him, and me, I couldn't find my way back.

I remember discovering Saint Anthony's Church. I think it was called St. Anthony's. At the church, I felt the first inkling of hope that I'd had in a long time.

There was a posting on the church office window advertising a job at a dairy farm. It invited interested people to come in and complete an application. I went in, not really expecting much. I had no experience with cows or farming. The notice seemed to indicate there was no experience necessary, so I took a chance.

I asked for an application, got one and filled it out. To my surprise, the worker told me to be at the church the following morning to meet my ride to the farm. I didn't say anything, but I was very happy. Here was a chance to make a start with a job and room and board. I was hoping this would be what I was looking for.

I practically camped out at the church to make sure I didn't miss my ride. Sure enough, a big cattle truck pulled up in front of the church. This was my ride. There was a small place in the back where there was enough room for one person. They advised me to be careful, as the ride was long and bumpy. I didn't care. I was on my way to a better place.

The ride was uneventful, somewhat cold, and definitely bumpy. At last, the truck stopped, and they opened the door so I could climb out. I really don't remember much about how the place looked. There really isn't any impression in my memory. If I'd stayed longer I might have some memory of the farm.

I was told to go in and someone would be with me to show me where I would stay. It was nice inside. It was warm and clean and I remember meeting some of the other farm hands. They seemed like a nice bunch of guys.

I put my belongings in a locker in my new room and made up my bed. There wasn't much unpacking to do, as I didn't have more than two coats and the clothes on my back. I was already feeling better when I was called to attend dinner. We had pizza and I had a hot cup of steaming coffee. This was great.

Afterward, the headman called me into his office to discuss my paperwork and application. As he started to speak, I got the feeling all was not well. He brought up the part of my application where I'd written I had schizophrenia. He then began talking about how the farm was not prepared to handle persons with mental illness and they had no recourse but to ask me to leave. I was crushed, and wasn't able to hide my tears. I was to leave the next morning for a ride back to San Francisco.

I arrived in the city the next morning, and began what was to be the darkest and most desolate time of my life. I wandered aimlessly for days. I would sleep where I could find space. I would eat when I could remember where the soup kitchens were. I wasn't drinking or doing drugs at this time. I couldn't get my spirits up high enough to try to panhandle. Things had gone from bad to really worse.

I would find a place to sleep and wake up with the police telling me to move on. That happened several times. Since there was no warrant for my arrest, they simply moved me from place to place. I think if they could have, they would've taken me to a hospital, but I wasn't sick in an obvious way. I had no outward signs other than my terrible appearance. They couldn't have known I was mentally ill.

One night I fell asleep in the Pan Handle, under a tree. I thought I'd found a spot where I could finally rest. There were no people around and the weather that night was a little warmer. So, I passed out and went into a deep sleep. I remember having a dream of being in the rain and thanked my lucky stars it was only a dream. I woke some time later to discover the park sprinklers had come on and I was thoroughly soaked, and terribly cold.

I did the only thing I could. I got up and walked around until I was dry. I was still cold and hungry. I think the worst part of this ordeal was the isolation and loneliness. When I looked up at the world, all I saw was a place with no room in it for me. I believed there was no end to this loneliness and the pain would continue until I finally died. I began to think of death as the solution, and I hoped that I would die soon.

I wandered for some time; I'm not sure how long. I do remember having a significant thought. For some unknown reason I thought of trying to find psychiatric help. I figured maybe I could get inpatient treatment somewhere and end up with shelter and food for a while.

I asked someone where the county hospital was and got directions to San Francisco General Hospital. I thought maybe I could get some help and get started on a good path there.

I went in and got hooked up with a nurse. The nurse was somewhat skeptical of my story and seemed reluctant to do anything. I was able to convince her to contact a hospital in Indiana where I'd had numerous treatments. They seemed reluctant at first, but eventually they did it.

That hospital was able to verify my identity and that I did in fact have a diagnosis. This put them in a position to provide some help; although, the help was not exactly what I wanted.

I was informed that I could not get an inpatient bed, as they were full. They also suggested getting on a waiting list for a halfway house. The wait for the halfway house was about a month, but I was sure I would be dead before that.

They did get me a meal and a 30-day supply of psychiatric medication. The meal was good and I hoped the medication would help. I left the hospital, but I didn't really feel much better. It seemed to me that another door had been closed. As I left the hospital, I began to think of suicide again.

Chapter 7

I've always existed. The only possible way reality can be real is if someone has always been there to be real. I've created and destroyed universes. I've brought nations to greatness and destroyed them on a whim. I have created worlds within worlds, microcosms to endless expanses of space.

There has been no age in which my awareness has not played a part. There has been no god that has ruled without my first creating that god and bestowing the necessary power. I have created the omnipotent god from nothing. I have made the most ghastly creations into the most angelic of all to behold.

I created a devil to give me sport. I have used this creature to stimulate my mind, and present to me a challenge. I have warred with this devil for many ages. I never cease to be amused by his determination to overthrow me. I am not merciless to this poor wretch. I do offer pardon and a way out of his predicament from time to time. I do believe that I have hurt him badly enough to have caused him to hate so much that he may continue to refuse redemption and opt for continuous war. Of course, this would only happen if I let it happen.

I have had many challenges from servants who doubt my trueness. They have issued many trials. Asking me to complete these tasks to prove I am who I am. I have always succeeded. There has not been one test that I have failed.

I butted in on God as he was creating Adam and Eve. I tried to tell Him that it wouldn't work. I tried to stop Him, but he wouldn't have any of it. I told Him that if He give a creature free will, don't expect that creature to behave as you dictate. After all, if one is truly free, then one is not ruled by others. If you are free then there is no power that can claim you as servant.

I'm always amused by how the servant population seems to equate their standing as servants with freedom. It is quite humorous. I sometimes think God put that notion in his slaves to entertain me. Of course, it could be that if these servants of God discovered the truth they would realize they really are free, and have no need of God.

God fights hard to keep his slaves. I don't think he realizes how much fun He could have if He didn't have a bunch of people to take care of.

At this point it might be wise to remind you that you are reading something written by a person with a complex delusional self-belief system. I would like to continue my divergence into the entire delusion, but that would be impossible. I can't start at the beginning, there isn't one. I can't explain an ending because there isn't one. This book is not about my delusions. This book is about finding hope and learning the promise of love.

There are many tails of drunkenness, and psychotic revelations. I feel that it would be wrong, at this time, to relate funny stories about my escapades. I don't want the reader to feel that alcoholism and mental illness are things that someone chooses. I hope the reader can see that getting rid of these illnesses is something quite beyond the ability to will oneself to wellness. If that were the case, I would have cured myself years ago.

That's how I got to this point of wanting to die again. All of these things are pieces of the puzzle of my life. All of my experience has been culminated into one moment. It is in this moment that I chose to step forward. It was in this lost and desolate universe that I decided to step into the future — to stop running, to learn to look up and to keep putting one foot in front of the other no matter what happens.

As I contemplated suicide, and rejected suicide, this is where I found myself. I found my courage. I shed the thought of escape and started a journey out of darkness and into a place of hope.

It would be some years before I could understand the impact of this choice. I was not to realize a quick and painless recovery. But, it has been in recovery that I've discovered the true strength of my decisions to keep moving forward.

I found that it is immensely important to focus on hope and gratitude. It is the power of the human spirit to believe that there is a point to our lives and that we can find these things that brings us the real value. There is Faith, Hope and Charity, and the greatest of these is Love.

Somehow, the decision to make progress was a defining moment in my life. I can look back on those experiences and find amazing instances of miracles not of my doing. It is with compassion that I will do my best to show you the path that has led me out of darkness.

I believe that the concept of putting one foot in front of the next does more than propel one along a path. I believe this attitude will determine how much or how little progress will be made. It is in retrospect that I find strength coming from that first decision to move forward. I do, at times, continue to put one foot forward, as life can still be difficult.

My journey from darkness has given me a new hope for a better tomorrow. I can see a place where life can truly be lived. And, I believe that I can be in that place should I choose to do what is right.

I'm still in a deplorable state. I haven't bathed in some time. I know I must smell awful, and look worse. Now that I've decided no matter what I will move on, I find myself looking up. I feel as though I've broken through to the other side. I feel stronger.

In my moment of hope, I decide to go to Los Angeles. My thinking is that it's bigger and there must be more opportunity to make money here. At least that is my thought.

In deciding to move on, I realized I had no money for bus fare. I decided to visit the Travelers Aid Society to see if I could get a ticket from them. The fellow at the Society was really nice and helpful. He asked for my identification and asked me to wait. As I waited, I felt somewhat uneasy, but I know now I must do what I must do, so I wait.

After a little while, he called me into his office. He talked to me and said going to Los Angeles was a bad idea. He felt it was unsafe for someone whose faculties are not quite up to speed.

The bomb he dropped had nothing to do with the bus ticket. During the course of doing a background check on me, he had somehow gotten in touch with my parents and it seemed he had quite a conversation.

He explained that my parents would fly me home if I agreed to stay clean and sober and stay on my medication. At this point, I'd been clean for a couple of days and I had fresh supply of medication, so I agreed to their terms. I was happy for a chance to try again.

I had to hang around San Francisco for a couple of days while arrangements for a bus ticket to LAX and my plane ticket were finalized. I had the first shower in a while, and I had a room and coupons for McDonalds. I was living well.

I bought some food and then was able to get cigarettes with the change. I remember feeling unsure of my future, but feeling very good about things now.

Don't get on the bandwagon just yet. There were still many obstacles to overcome. It was going to take me years to recover, and I had only just begun.

I don't remember much of the ride to Los Angeles. It was uneventful. I didn't speak to anyone, and I don't remember if any one spoke to me. I had a kind of empty feeling where my stomach should have been. I didn't want to admit it, but I was thoroughly beaten down. Even so, I was determined to stick to this new path.

The only thing I remember about the flight to Indianapolis International was the poor guy who had to sit next to me on the plane. I had bathed, sure, but I had not washed my clothes. I apologized, but the fellow seemed inclined to ignore me. He did pay attention when I asked for cigarette, though. As a matter of fact he gave me a whole pack. That sure was grand of him.

Later, as I thought more about it, I think he hoped I would keep a cigarette lit the whole time to help mask the smell of gutter that hung so heavily on me. It must have bothered everyone near me.

As I disembarked from the plane, I was at another turning point. I wondered if I should follow through with meeting my parents. As luck would have it, I saw them before they saw me. I decided to follow them a while and think some more about what I was going to do.

They didn't notice me following them, but as I did, I reached a conclusion. I decided to put one foot in front of the next and try to figure out the right thing to do. In this case, the right thing to do was to greet them and go home. So, that's what I did.

The ride home in the car was rather quiet. My relationship with my family was really strained by this time. I found that even trying to say the right things was awkward at best. I sensed maybe they weren't sure about having me there. I admit I had been a handful in the past and had a good record of fouling things up on a regular basis.

They had a surprise for me. I was informed I was going to the Mental Health Hospital for inpatient care. There was going to be a medication adjustment. I believe my mother and father needed assurance that I was on medication and could be stabilized.

I'm sure they felt there was little they could do for me. I know that my mother spent many years praying for me.

There are times when I believe her prayers kept me alive and in God's good grace.

There was one more surprise in store for me. I was not going to be able to go home after discharge from the hospital. My father thought maybe it was time for me to sink or swim. I was going to have to learn to stand on my own two feet. The difference this time was I agreed with him.

I now realized my life was my responsibility and there were certain issues I needed to address. Independence was starting to look different to me. I was beginning to see that I needed to stick with things and follow through.

The experience at the hospital was different this time around. It seemed the staff had become enlightened. There was more talk of my taking an active role in my life. There was the issue of my drug and alcohol use that needed attention, though.

I think medical science must've progressed rapidly in the '80s, because the staff seemed to recognize all of my little manipulations and cons. It could be I was a little more sober and able to see that others could see through my façade easier than I had believed previously.

I was put on a medication that seemed to work to help me stay calm. The medications used back then didn't work like the effective treatments we have now. Being able to stay calm and not act on every impulse was, at that time, considered effective treatment.

During one interview with a psychiatrist I admitted I had a drug and alcohol problem, so it was off to drug rehab for me. This was the first drug rehab treatment for me. I must admit that it did help for a while.

After discharge, I stayed clean and sober for about nine months. This is saying a lot. I think I began to have real fun, though. I remember many times fellowshipping with other drunks and many fun evenings drinking coffee and making jokes.

I believe these experiences of enjoying life, being with others, and making progress did something to me. I began to think that life without drugs or alcohol could be enjoyable and rewarding. This was quite a thought for the person I was then.

For many years, my life had been all about me. Now, I was thinking along the lines of maybe, just maybe, I had some hope to offer someone else. I began to seriously consider what it was going to take for me to stay clean and sober.

Somehow, though, I found myself drinking and smoking pot, again. I don't know how it happened. I was convinced I was an alcoholic and I really wanted to quit. I had finally realized what the disease was doing to me, and I had been going to a lot of AA meetings. I was sure that AA was supposed to work to keep me sober. I was completely baffled by the fact that in spite of all my efforts, I was drinking again.

Through the years, I had always maintained that since I never spent rent money or grocery money on booze I was somehow not that bad. Not to mention that through the years, every time I was hospitalized or homeless, it was directly related to my alcoholism. But, I also thought I'd been good about paying my bills.

This time things were worse. I remember sitting at the kitchen table in my low rent hovel. As I drank, I realized I had spent all of my money on alcohol, and there wasn't any left for the rent or for food. An odd thing happened then. I convinced my self I would go into to treatment for a month, until my next check came. I knew all the right words, and I was sure they would let me in.

I was right. The next morning, I met with the people at the hospital and got myself checked into the rehab center. This time, things were different here, too. I was to complete the program and be on my way. It was clearly shown to me that I was not to return to this hospital.

Once I finished the twenty-eight day treatment, I was going to have to leave for good. The doctor pointed out that I'd had numerous inpatient treatments there, and it seemed they weren't helping me. I was told that if I returned after this stint, I would be institutionalized at a state hospital for at least one year. I never went back there as a patient.

I was still playing games, somewhat. At my discharge, I decided to forego getting an apartment and would spend all my money on drugs and alcohol. I figured I could afford more booze if I didn't have rent to pay. The weather was nice, so it seemed like a good idea. I was expecting some good drunks and a carefree life. All of this was coming from some one who had been homeless because of excess drinking.

I did pretty well for about three days. The money ran out much quicker than I expected. I was baffled again, and wondered what I did wrong this time. I was not having much luck.

About a month later I finally got an apartment and tried to settle in. I'd developed a bad habit of spending all my money on parties, so I was always looking for food and cigarettes. I also hooked up with a very good woman and we seemed to hit things off pretty well.

About two weeks after we met, we moved in together and began a romance that would last for about three years. We decided to help each other stay sober and were positive about making a life together.

We both relapsed a number of times. We would threaten each other, saying, "If you use you lose." We thought we were on the right track.

At one point, she went into treatment because she needed it. At this time, I'd been sober for a few months and was feeling pretty strong. I don't know what happened, but I was drinking before she returned from rehab.

Consequently, I was drunk when she got back. Boy was she unhappy with me. She laid down the law and that meant treatment for me. I couldn't go back to my usual haunt — they'd threatened to lock me up for good. So, I went out of town and spent about thirty days in a different rehab center.

During the treatment, a staff psychologist stopped my antipsychotic medications. He believed my core problem was the substance addictions, not mental illness. So, I was stark raving sober upon discharge.

Again, I was determined that I was going to be clean and sober for the rest of my life. This was going to be my turning point. Are you starting to understand that no matter where I went, or who I was with, I was not in control?

I left the center with a good attitude and the internal belief that I could stay clean and sober. I thought I would make a fresh start and stay in good shape. I was in love, too. That made things seem better. I hadn't had much experience with the opposite sex, and I was really enjoying myself. I was with a good woman who loved me back.

I got a job right out of treatment. It wasn't a high paying job, but I was making a new path in life for myself. Things really started to look good.

Soon after I began this endeavor, my girlfriend experienced something terrible. It was something that changed her attitude and outlook on life. It also showed me that I had a serious anger problem.

As the dust settled, it became apparent that the best thing to do was have my girlfriend return to her parents' house. It seemed like a good way to help her recover. It also was a good way for me to go somewhere else. Somewhere where my past might leave me alone.

We packed up and moved to a new state. We were ready to start anew. I was going to stay with her family until I could find my own place.

I managed to locate an apartment to move into quickly. I also secured employment. The transition was going pretty smooth.

I was going to AA regularly and I was working the steps with a sponsor. I was getting caught up on my bills, and started to feel pretty good about things.

I'd been sober for almost a year when the decision to stop my medications came back to haunt me. I'd been working at a fast food joint to supplement my income. I was doing well. I got a couple of raises and was promoted twice.

But, it was not to be the good thing I'd planned for. My psychotic symptoms returned full force. They were worse than ever. I was hallucinating almost constantly, and when I wasn't hallucinating, I was sitting staring into space like a zombie.

I had many excursions into the unreal. I fought demons and the devil. I challenged God and sought to gain power over the angels. As I sat in my own mess, I ruled the worlds and paid no heed to caution.

The problem was, while I was doing this, I wasn't eating or bathing. I was in a bad way and I desperately needed help.

I must say that I am eternally grateful to my girlfriend for sticking by me during this time. She was able to assure the doctors I would start my medications again. She had everything to do with my recovery from this psychosis. I think that without her attention, I would have ended up in a sanitarium for a long time.

During this period of recovery, I lived with my girlfriend and her parents. I was stable on medications and had been clean and sober for about nine months. I remember she said she believed I would never drink again. I wasn't as hopeful as she was, though. I thought I still wasn't catching on to this sobriety concept, and I was right.

In retrospect I can see this was truly a good beginning in recovery. For now, I could see I didn't understand, and that sobriety was going to be elusive. It is often said that one must surrender to gain victory. I see too that one needs to realize the situation is hopeless before one can see the need for help.

It was at this time I decided to return to my family in Indiana. With a fair degree of manipulation, I convinced my parents to let me move in with them. I made the usual agreement that there would be no drug or alcohol use while I was there. I remember I finally agreed that I had some serious problems that would take time to overcome. It was going to longer than I had imagined.

Chapter 8

There really weren't very many significant events during this time in my life. I continued to smoke marijuana and drink. I continued my usual curmudgeonly behavior. I had come full circle. I was at a point where I believed I would not have a life — there would be no career or normal life for me.

I spent time traveling back and forth from Indiana to my girlfriend's place. This went on for about six months. It was then that I broke off our relationship. I decided I would not be able to keep my commitment to her and it would be better to break it off instead of putting more years into something that would ultimately fail.

I spent a lot of time hiding my drinking and doping. I'm not sure if my parents ever knew I was drinking almost everyday. I was certainly getting high at every opportunity. I was also ruining any chance at building friendships. I had resigned myself to the fact that the best I could manage would be to live on my disability check and welfare.

The seed of sobriety had been planted in my soul. I was considering what it would take to get sober. These last ten years had been painful and confusing.

I would have times of wanting to stay sober and being unsuccessful. I would have times when sobriety didn't matter and would immerse myself in drugs and alcohol wishing reality would go away and not come back.

One day I received an unusual invitation in the mail. It was an application to attend training to become a Peer Advocate. I didn't know what a Peer Advocate was, but I completed the application and sent it back. My reaction was one of disbelief and I wondered how they'd gotten my name. I didn't think any more about it until I received a letter saying I'd been accepted for training.

This was to be the first in a series of events that were going to change the course of my life. I didn't realize I would soon be mixing with people who were just like me. These people were going to show me there was a way to live and that I could accomplish it.

I was somewhat excited about participating. I was going to Indianapolis to attend and that meant overnight stays and eating out. I've always liked to travel, and this time I would get to have food and room, too.

The training took two weeks and went rather well. I was able to focus and the lessons seemed to fall into place for me. I completed the training and was able to earn a Peer Advocate certificate.

After that, I returned to rural Indiana to continue to live with my parents. I didn't think too much more about the training I had completed. It could be noted that this was the only thing I'd completed since I earned my GED years earlier.

I stayed on the farm with my parents for a couple more years. My mother was heavily active as an advocate for the mentally ill. Having children with these issues has really been a learning experience for her. She was able to use that experience to support others and to advocate for those in need.

Her work took her away from the house consistently. She would usually spend the week in Indianapolis and return to the farm on the weekends.

There was a short period of time when my younger brother was living at home, too. We didn't hang out much. He'd gone to high school in the area and knew quite a few kids his own age. It seemed he was occupied most of the time with them.

My father was there and was still working at the same job. He would get up very early and drive to work. When he got home in the evening, he would sit up and watch TV after dinner.

It was my job to see to it that the house was kept in order. I cleaned and did laundry during the day. In the evenings, I had dinner ready when dad got home. I felt somewhat useful, as I was keeping the house in order and contributing to the well being of the family.

I was in that situation for a number of years. It seemed I could hold it together and manage those few simple tasks each day. I was still smoking marijuana regularly and was getting drunk on some days. I don't know if my parents had finally gotten to a point where they expected me to be using or if they were ignoring it.

I went to great lengths to hide my drinking and doping. I like to think that maybe I'd found a way to control myself a little better.

A few years in the future, I'd realize I didn't need drink or drugs. For now, though, I still used them as coping mechanisms.

I'd met a few people during this time, but I wasn't capable of building a true relationship with others. This being said, I haven't seen or heard anything about those good people for a long time.

The time came for my father to retire. He'd held a job for many years and was ready to assume a life of leisure. I always marveled at the fact that he'd worked the same job for 35 years. This used to really baffle me. I would often think, *How could anyone work for that long?*

We went about selling everything we did not need or want and prepared to move. We were moving to Indianapolis. I thought things were looking up. I was looking forward to the fact that it would be easier to get pot in a bigger city and I wouldn't have to walk eight miles in one direction to get a drink. So, with enthusiasm, I was ready to move to the city.

Our new house was in a nice neighborhood that was really attractive. It was next to the clubhouse and pool, so it wasn't far to go to lounge about in the summer and swim and enjoy the city.

I developed a routine of walking to the malls and bars and movie theatres. I was feeling pretty good. I felt like I was starting to calm down and relax. I even thought maybe I should get a part-time job so I'd have a little extra pocket money.

I don't know how it happened, but the place that trained me as an advocate called and told me there was a job opening in Indianapolis. If I took it, I'd be doing the Peer Advocacy I'd been trained for. I thought I'd give it a go and applied.

I was hired. Actually, I was more than hired. When I went to the interview, I expected to see something like a sheltered workshop or some kind of mental health program. Boy did I get an eyeful that day.

I was introduced to a number of people who said were glad to meet me. I hadn't heard that in a long time.

They also explained that they had mental illnesses, the same as me, and they were holding jobs or had their own businesses. The really remarkable thing was they hired me after the interview.

These people opened my eyes to a whole new world of possibilities. They showed me hope. They showed me something I hadn't felt for a long time. I owe these people a great deal. I do my best each day to reach out to my peers to offer them the same hope that was freely given to me.

I was still smoking a little now and then, and I'd drink a little, too. But, my desires for sobriety and freedom were beginning to gain power over the obsession to use and drink. I was starting to feel that when I was straight I was more normal. Undoubtedly my years of support group work were starting to payoff.

There was also another turning point at this time. Usually the medications I took really didn't do whole of good, and they all had some serious side effects. Even so, I continued treatment.

I also had a unique opportunity. I was selected to participate in a research program for people with schizophrenia. I was going to be on a new drug that was much more effective with fewer side effects.

I admit I had doubts at first, but my recent successes had already begun to increase my sense of well-being. I was willing to make the necessary commitment for the research. I had a very good doctor working with me. He was able to show me how to use the treatment and what to expect. He told me I needed to be willing to make a two-year commitment for the project.

I thought it over for about a week before finally agreeing to participate. I had nothing to lose, so I went for it. If the treatment did what the doctor claimed, then it was going to be worthwhile. If the treatment failed, then so what, I wasn't going to be out anything. Besides, I could save money on medication while I was in the project because the treatment was free.

The drug name was Clozaril, and it is now considered one of the best, if not *the* best, treatment for schizophrenia. The medication has also proved useful for treating several other mental health issues.

It was a pretty rigorous program. I had to have a weekly blood draw for a white blood cell count. This was necessary because a known side effect caused bone marrow to stop or greatly reduce white blood cell production. This can cause death, as a person can't fight off common diseases like the flu or even serious colds.

I picked up my medication up once a week. I could only get the prescription after my cell count was verified and deemed normal.

I must admit that while the side effects were fewer, there were still some serious issues. I experienced tremendous weight gain. In the first year of treatment, I went from 185 pounds to a whopping 298 pounds. This was because the medication made me feel hungry, so I ate much more than usual. The medication also had a sedating effect, which caused me to sleep a great deal. Put both of those problems to together and we're talking some serious weight changes.

I also drooled in my sleep. I would soak a pillow pretty good at night and wake to find my head in a small puddle on the bed.

Why did I stick with the treatment through all of this? Well, I was beginning to experience things I hadn't experienced for many years.

I made a few friends — real friends, not like before. Before I only hung around others when I wanted something. Now, I was starting to find that just being around people for the sake of being good company was worthwhile. It also seemed these new friends liked to be around me, and they didn't have ulterior motives.

I'd taken the job as a Peer Advocate, and was able to show up for work and do my job. I'd never held a job for more than a month or so previously, but I held this job for two years. During that time, I was beginning to find out my peers were okay with me being in positions of authority.

I was surprised when my coworkers nominated me to the position of Vice-President of the Board. I was even more surprised to hear, in my own voice, that I would accept. The clincher came when I was elected. These good people had enough faith in me to trust me like this. I was finally going to take this seriously. I was just beginning to see that this real life I'd found was taking a turn for the better.

My first official act as VP was to secede the President of the Board. Early in my first term, the President passed away. This was sorrowful, as this man had befriended me. He was a man of courage and strength. It was going to be very difficult to follow in his path, and I was afraid of failure. I thought that maybe I should step down.

But, deep in my heart I decided I was going to do my best to lead this organization as best I could. This was another milestone for me. I didn't cut and run the way I usually did. I was beginning to show character.

I continued to work as a Peer Advocate, as well as leading the Board. I was, during this time, evaluating my own commitment toward sobriety and responsibility. I found that with the proper medication, I no longer I had the over powering urge to drink or use drugs.

The help I received from peers and support groups also played an important role. I showed up for work on time, and I followed through with completing the Board work in a professional manner. I must admit, I was flying in the dark a lot. What did I know about leadership? I was the guy that everyone stayed away from. But, here I was being responsible and acting right.

I've been able to continue to serve this organization, and have spent many years on the board. I've always used the cause of helping others to guide me. This goal has not faded from my thoughts. I want to be able to give others the hope and strength that was given to me.

After my first term as President, I was elected again, and I served again. I was elected to lead the board for the next five years. I also continued to work as a staff member for two more years.

The Executive Director gave me her support and encouragement, and I decided to resign as Peer Advocate and return to school. I remained active in the leading the Board, but began a new path to better myself and to try to access better opportunity.

It was a time when I felt that things in life that used to scare me into running or would paralyze me with fear were losing their strength. I was looking at an uncertain future with fear, yes, but also with courage and hope.

I set off on my way to college. My memories of school weren't all that positive and I felt this was going to be a real challenge. I hadn't completed a homework assignment in over twenty years, and I knew I was going to be the oldest person in the classes. But, I stayed the course and put my fears aside.

I was soon found the other students were friendly enough, and I wasn't the oldest student there. I also managed to impress my instructors. I decided I would only reveal my schizophrenia and alcoholism if it became necessary. I never experienced a situation where it became necessary to divulge that, though I did sneak it in during my abnormal psychology studies. I thought it would be humorous to surprise my professor at the end of those classes. So, that's what I did.

In my final paper I included my own experience with abnormal psych came from the fact that I had my very own abnormal psych. The professor was surprised by this and said I hid it well. I didn't have the heart to tell him I wasn't hiding it. I just never brought it up.

I was invited by this professor to return and present my story to his other classes. I think I'd still be helping him teach if he was still in that position.

I was beginning to experience a better life. Before graduation from college, I was clean and sober. To this date, I've been sober for over twenty-three years. I haven't used street drugs for more twenty-six years. I'm getting better.

A friend nominated me for the "Men of the Year" award in the National Registry of Outstanding Americans. I was surprised by that. I received this acknowledgement very early in my sobriety and clean time. It was unexpected to say the least, and a nice surprise, even though I did not win an award.

I was asked to serve on the Board of Directors of the Depressive/Manic Depressive Organization. After two years as a member at large, I was elected Vice-President of the board. After a few years there, I resigned and have not gone back. I've just been too busy, and I've had to pick my battles carefully.

I graduated college with high honors. I successfully finished a two-year degree in just three years. I spent a few summer breaks fishing, and was able to teach a friend how to fish. We went on some interesting excursions and really had a blast. I was able to open up to another person for the first time in a long time. My friend helped more than he can know.

On graduation day, I received the best gift my father ever gave me. We had a short conversation in which, with a tear in his eye, he told me he was proud of me. He gave me a big hug and told me he loved me. I still get a little teary-eyed when I think of it.

After this, I realized I needed something better than welfare and a disability check. I learned that being mentally ill has its problems, but I still have talents and abilities. It was a matter of trying to find the right place to use those skills. So, I began a job hunt. I was going to work my way off of the disabled list and get a life.

It was also scary. I had relied on that check for so long that going to work sounded like a big undertaking. I had many questions. I didn't want to fail and end up back on the streets. I'd been there and I was *not* going back.

I was at the Peer Advocate office and happened to notice a job posting there. It was for something called a Peer Counselor. The posting included a contact number and instructions for applying. I thought a Peer Counselor couldn't be much different from a Peer Advocate, plus I had a brand new college degree as a Substance Abuse Counselor, so I gave it a shot. I applied and waited.

A couple of days later, I received a call for an interview. I thought, *Okay, so far so good.* I scheduled a time to go and I made it there on time. The interview seemed pretty intense, and I was sure my lack of work experience was going to end up being a problem. I was also sure my drug and alcohol problem was going to end my chances.

But, I was worried over nothing. I was asked back for a second and third interview, and was hired shortly after. I had my first professional job that paid more than minimum wage.

The people I worked with went to great lengths to help me learn the system and all of its technical difficulties. They were patient and supportive of me, and I think I surprised them when I was able to do the job without constant supervision.

My job entailed going into the community and meeting with patients in their homes to talk about how they could get better. My message was simple. Use the treatment to cope, instead of no treatment or drugs and alcohol.

Many times, I would work with people who had been down and out for years. These were people who were exactly where I'd been. I worked with people who had lost sight of their dreams, just as I had done. I took my message of hope to them and showed them there is a way.

I talked to them about overcoming problems and realizing they could manage. I know I helped a couple of people, and they gave me much more than I'd ever got from a paycheck. They were teaching me about life and about what being knocked down repeatedly can do to a person.

I knew from my own experiences what it was like to be sick and full of symptoms. This new job showed me how to help someone else who was in that awful place, and what great effort it took to get out of there. Getting out of the darkness is not easy — not for them, and not for me.

After a year working part-time, I was offered a full-time position as a regular case manager. I readily accepted the challenge and immediately set out to work my way off of disability and welfare. This was another scary thing. I'd had a steady income from Social Security for about thirteen years. It was never enough money, but I never worried about losing the income and it was always there.

I was taking a big step, and it had me worried for awhile. Most of my worry came from the idea that I was going to have to pay for my own medication and treatment. My part in the research program was finished and I was no longer eligible for free services there.

My treatment was costly, what with having blood work done once every week and buying medication it cost about $480 per month. That was a lot of money. It would be three months before my insurance from work would take effect.

I decided this opportunity might be my only chance to stand on my own, so I went ahead and took the job. I nearly went bankrupt those first three months, but I made it.

After the insurance started picking up the cost of my treatment, I had another first. I was able to buy a small truck and didn't need a cosigner. I'd always wanted to do that. Being financially independent wasn't something homeless people believed in on a day-to-day basis, so this was big for me.

The blessing of insurance coverage was short lived. After a couple of years, my premium skyrocketed. I found myself paying a high premium as well as large co-pays. It got to a point where I was paying about 80% of the cost. I felt a little helpless, and was worried because I had more money going out than coming in.

I finally went to the Veteran's Hospital. I was a veteran and had used VA services before. The reason I hadn't gone there first resort was because for some time they hadn't paid for any treatment I was on. As I investigated their services, I found that they had begun to cover my treatment. Now, I no longer needed insurance from my employer, and my co-pays at the VA were low cost and without a premium. This was such a relief.

I must add that with the help of spiritual advisors, family, friends and a lot of support I've achieved things that I had believe to be out of reach for me. I'm not doing badly for a guy with such a colorful past. I really am blessed that today I can give to others what was so freely given to me.

At my job I have the privilege to work with people who are just like me. I get to help them off of drugs and alcohol. Plus, I can help them understand why medications are important. I have, at times, been able to demonstrate that treatment works, and above all else, that life *is* attainable.

To me, having a job was a blessing. The many years of failed attempts had weighed heavy on me. I thought life was something one worked at, but never got quite right. Going from homelessness to hopefulness, and being able to use those experiences to make a living is truly remarkable.

Chapter 9

There were many days, weeks and sometimes months where, upon waking, I wished for death. I would curse myself for being born. I saw an endless landscape of despair that held no promise for me. How did I survive? How is it that I was able to be the person I am today?

Yesterday, I woke up early. It was a Saturday, a day off from work, and a time for rest and relaxation. Days off are for me. They are my time for rejuvenation.

I ate a light breakfast and got cleaned up. Then it was time to do some investigating. I went to a local car dealer to check out a sale. I drove down there in my brand new car. After speaking with a salesman I decided to hold off and not by another car. I could do it, but there was no reason to do it right now.

I drove back home, put the car up and got out my new motorcycle. It was cold, so I put on my cold weather gear and tore off down the road. I rode for a while and then returned home for lunch. After lunch I took a short nap.

Feeling refreshed upon waking, I took off on the motorcycle again. I rode for a couple of hours and then went home.

My brother and his wife came to dinner, and we had a nice visit. It was good to be with family. After dinner, I went to my support group meeting. I always go a few times each week. I feel it does a lot to help me focus on what's important. It also helps me to remember what I don't want to go back to.

I went home afterwards and played some video games. Then, it was off to bed. I was asleep soon after my head hit the pillow.

I've had some other notable accomplishments. I have a career and I can perform at a level where I contribute something positive to the situation. I have served on numerous boards and committees, and I continue to volunteer quite a bit. I enjoy this work of helping others.

I think the most important part of all of this for me is being able to use all of those dark and desperate experiences to benefit others. I can truly say that as I continue to help others, those experiences have become of immense value to me.

I tell you these things not to brag, but to say that I have a life today. Recovery is very real and obtainable. Life is a great and wonderful thing. I hope that my story can offer hope to those who know someone who is suffering. I hope this story can offer the sick hope for a good life.

Closing Thoughts

The past twenty-eight years have been years of blessings for me. I've had many firsts and some of my dreams have come true. There have been some down times, too. I've lost things that can't be replaced. But through the help of my God, family, friends, and those in the medical community who offer their help to me, I manage to live as a normal person.

I have a sibling who is a victim of mental illness. Her disease is every bit as bad as mine. Her symptoms have taken everything from her and they've taken her from her family.

I wish I knew what to do for her. She disappeared some time back, and hasn't tried to contact us. This is pretty hard on our mom. Mom has always held hope for all of her children, but in my sister's case, hoping has been hard and has been going on for a long time.

My Fathers' recent passing has also added a lot to the picture. My parents were married for a long time. It was hard on all of us, but we know it has really been hard for Mom.

There are a lot of things in my life today — some are good and some are bad. My life is like most other people's now. That's really saying something. It's a great comfort to me to know I can live a normal life, and that I can handle the good with the bad.

A particular individual who has been an inspiration to me once told me the fact is, I could get sick again. The medication might stop working or I could develop other problems. If I do become ill again, I'll know what to do. I've been in treatment for so long now, the system is familiar to me. I know where to go and what to do.

If I use what I've learned through the many years of treatment and continue to use my support system, I'll be able to have a satisfactory life. I might even win the lottery, you never know.

It is hard to balance things sometimes. There are things that go on in the world that I don't understand. Sometimes, there are things that go on that I wish I didn't understand. The greatest thing for me is being in a position to help others. Helping others get their lives in order has been such a great experience. Granted, it can be heartbreaking to see someone struggle and not make it out of the darkness, but ultimately helping is worth it.

To all those Social Workers, Therapists, Doctors, and Counselors out there — I am the one you helped. I am the one person who was able to use all that you gave to help me live. I know now what hard work and dedication you demonstrate everyday, as I, too, have joined the ranks of those who give so others may live. I believe we are the chosen ones. Without our efforts, there would be no way out of the darkness.

My story will continue for as long as I live, and I will live for as long as I am supposed to. If I continue to do what is right, there is still no guarantee of health or wealth, but then there doesn't have to be.

It's been 12 years since the preceding chapters were penned. There have been many times in those years that required hard work and perseverance.

I've thought about what I would add to my story today. I still find it difficult to impress on others the depth of my gratitude. I would like to be able to express that life is worthwhile and is a treasure. I feel there is so much to say about mental health recovery, and addiction recovery.

I have read that pain is the touchstone of spiritual growth. I have read that experience has no substitute. My experiences were at one point very painful. In those years I would not believe I was growing spiritually. I did not put much value to my experiences.

I see now that life is to be lived. Dreams are to be followed. Peace is to be sought after. Understanding and grace should be given to each person in equal measure. There is no one else. There is only us. We all share the same world.

Sometimes, I can relate to someone because of shared pain. In these instances I do my best to share the solutions. To be understanding and to be hopeful.

I can make comparisons about my past and my present. I can share my dreams for the future. Yet, somehow it seems incredibly difficult to convey the message of Hope.

From destitution to fulfillment. From desperate loneliness to family and friends. From extreme isolation to an important connection to the world. From an outlook of pain and torment to a life that is full of light and Hope. All of these are part of my experience.

My life today seems to be the same contradiction it has always been. It used to be how can things become so terrible? Today, life is good, but through all of that there are problems and tough times.

I claim my life today is great, and it is more than I ever thought it would be. The real gift is being able to walk with my head held high. Clean and sober and sane.

See you around!

www.ingramcontent.com/pod-product-compliance
Lightning Source LLC
Chambersburg PA
CBHW070055120526
44588CB00033B/1549